THE SAGA OF THE 1ST FIGHTER CONTROL SQUADRON

Memories of Our History

Compiled by

TOM GAUTHIER

For the Veterans
Who Lived and Died For It

From the work of
Chester W. Driest (1920-1999)

Published by
ToMar Associates Publishing
Janesville, California

The Saga of the
1ˢᵗ Fighter Control Squadron
Memories of Our History

Copyright 2015 by Tom Gauthier

Based on the work of Chester Driest
With attributions as listed in the bibliography

This book is based on the personal memoirs and historic
notations contained in the 1995 collections of Chester Driest
and additional historical material.

Cover design by Ray White
Author Photo by Pam Woodworth

"Corporal Chester Zaborowski designed a logo for the
squadron clubhouse on Mindoro.
The squadron adopted his design as their insignia in 1944."

ISBN-13: 978-0692432709
ISBN-10: 0692432701

Printed in the United States of America

NOTE: PHOTOGRAPHS USED THROUGHOUT THIS BOOK
ARE FROM CHESTER DRIEST'S COLLECTION AND ARE
REPRINTED AS RECEIVED. THEY ARE FROM ORIGINALS,
UNRETOUCHED, AND IN WHATEVER CONDITION THEY
SURVIVED FROM 1943-45.

Dedicated

To
Chester W. Driest
(1920-1999)

And
The Men of
The 1st Fighter Control Squadron
Who Lost Their Lives in the Sinking of the
Troopship USAT Cape San Juan,
11 November 1943

Cpl Wilbur A. Barger	**Oregon**
Sgt Edmund A. Cannon	**Minnesota**
Sgt James O. Clowdus	**Alabama**
Cpl William L. Darsey	**California**
Cpl Richard P. Hergenrother	**Pennsylvania**
PFC Benjamin Keen	**Michigan**
2nd Lt Stanley O. McDonald	**Texas**
PFC Charles E. Miner	**Connecticut**
PFC Rosario A. Mocciaro	**New York**
Cpl Max F. Wilkans	**Illinois**

Missler, Wm J. (KIA 1944)

ACKNOWLEDGEMENTS

My work is compiler—not writer—of this unit history of the 1st Fighter Control Squadron in the South Pacific during World War II. The contributions of many people make this book possible.

First, of course, is Chester Driest himself. Back in 1996 he was kind enough to make me an honorary member of the 1st Fighters—and provide me a copy of his compilation *From L.A. To Luzon—With a Slight Pause off Fiji.* (See author's notes for the full story).

With the passing of Chet, the families of these warriors stepped up when I sought to write this book. Chet's daughter, Edie Driest, became invaluable in locating other original documents and photographs. She has become a friend, and I'm forever grateful for her help and support.

Thanks also to the son of Donald A. Dake, the commanding officer (for most of the war), Dr. Michael Dake, MD, who provided information and photos that are critical to the story.

The Bonfoey family, likewise, has supported the effort with pictures and information about their father, Captain Edward Monroe Bonfoey, who played a key role in the successful mission of this unit.

My thanks to Eric Stone, the intrepid researcher of the ships and men that played a pivotal role in the history of the 1st Fighters. A visit to www.ssarkansan.com, Eric's research website, is a voyage into the history of the Maritime Service in WWII.

Always a key player in producing my books, my friend Dr. Ray White, once again designed and executed the cover that is the first thing a reader sees. Thank you, Ray!

Finally, out of order of importance, thanks to my wife, Marlene, for her impeccable typing skills and readings, and for keeping me focused when I lose track of time in the office.

"Build me a son, O Lord, who will be strong enough to know when he is weak, and brave enough to face himself when he is afraid, one who will be proud and unbending in honest defeat, and humble and gentle in victory."

General Douglas MacArthur (1880-1964)

Table of Contents

Foreword
The Challenge   1

Introduction
3

Chapter One

Inception of the 1st Fighter Control Squadron   5
Headed for War   11

Chapter Two

History of Aircraft Interception
and Early Warning Systems   12

Chapter Three

Disaster at Sea—First Taste of Battle and Casualties
Ship Sinking Casualties   18
Survivors Taken To Noumea, Suva—and on to
Brisbane, Australia   60
First War Assignment—Finschhafen   63

Chapter Four

Battle of Hollandia (Operation Reckless)   67

Chapter Five

Battle of Wakde (Operation Straight Line   81
New Commanding Officer: Donald A. Dake   91

Chapter Six

Invasion of Leyte, Philippine Islands   100

Chapter Seven

Landing on Mindoro, Philippine Islands   104

Chapter Eight

Operations on Laoag and Lingayen   129

Roster

1st Fighter Control Squadron
Compiled from fragments from ship's roster   135

Biographies

Captain Edward Bonfoey   143
T/Sgt Chester Driest   145
Major Donald A. Dake   147

Authors Notes   150

Bibliography   152

Foreword

1ST FIGHTER CONTROL SQUADRON

The Challenge

How do you write a history of a WWII military unit when the official records of that unit lie at the bottom of the Pacific Ocean some three hundred miles from Fiji?

The answer involves some serendipity, some luck, and the tenacity of one man to rebuild the story of his, and his comrades' war experiences.

This group of men organized for a unique mission, and share a unique story. Most of their casualties occurred *on the way* to the Pacific War—and every member of the unit was awarded the Purple Heart. Only through the efforts of one of their own can we finally write this book in their honor and their memory.

Is it a history? Is it a memoir? Yes. It is the personal memories of the men intertwined with the recorded history of a WWII Pacific Campaign. Quoted from the memorial plaque at Wright-Patterson Air Force Base: "Initially torpedoes and

1

almost destroyed, the squadron rose from disaster to top performance of its control mission in the air war of the Pacific."

In 1995 a member of the 1ˢᵗ Fighter Control Squadron, Chester W. Driest, who personally lived every minute of this story, painstakingly collected and edited a collection of scattered, but related government records, and personal memoirs from his comrades, into a piece he titled:

From L.A. To Luzon—With a Slight Pause off Fiji

The title is telling in that Sergeant Driest and his comrades-in-arms experienced war, suffering, and death before they ever reached the battle zone during that … *Slight Pause off Fiji.* The reference is to the torpedo sinking of the troopship *SS Cape San Juan* on 11 November 1943 off the coast of the island of Fiji.

Chester W. Driest passed away in March 1999. His honored memory lives on. Thank you, sir, for helping me with my dream and for adding one more memorial to the memory of your comrades in arms. I know how important that was to you. I dedicate the first book to Chester, as I do this unit history based on his hard work.

Chester Driest

Introduction

"Initially torpedoed and almost destroyed, the squadron rose from disaster to top performance of its control mission in the air war of the Pacific."

"Sharks tore bodies from partially submerged life rafts in their hunger for human flesh. Some of the sharks had already made off with screaming men, and the blood from the bodies of those boys attracted more sharks. There were schools of them, I don't know how many, but they were seven to ten feet long—they even pulled men off rafts.

"All this time the water was infested with men on rafts, men clinging to wreckage, and men just swimming. The sharks were already there. Some of the rafts were partly submerged, and I saw men actually pulled off by the sharks.

"On one of the trips over I saw an Army captain going down and a shark circling around him. I dove overboard and got the captain into our boat. We got him aboard ship and he had a pint of whiskey on him. We didn't have a drop of whiskey on the ship, but this captain would not share a drink with us—said he was saving it."

4

Chapter One

The Inception of the 1st Fighter Control Squadron

(The following report, part of Chester Driest's compilation, was edited from a memorandum dated 4 June 1944 from Captain Rhinehart H. Miller, historical officer and squadron adjutant, to Commanding General of the Army Air Forces, Washington, DC.)

Initial Assembly, Organization, Training

The original designation of the unit when it was activated on 13 January 1942 at Selfridge Field, Michigan, was the *1st Interceptor Control Squadron*. The *Second Air Force* issued the General Order directing the activation of the unit and its assignment to the *First Pursuit Group*. The initial *TO&E* (Table of Organization and Equipment) called for seven officers and two hundred and eighty enlisted men.

The first soldier assigned to the unit was Sergeant Marcus J. Blome. He came from the 4th Air Base Squadron Headquarters, Selfridge Field, on orders dated 13 January 1942. He later became first sergeant of the organization. The first commanding officer, 2nd Lieutenant John C. Stoltze, reported on 21 January 1942. The day before, fifty enlisted soldiers reported to the unit. They came from the Air Corps replacement Training Center, Sheppard Field, Texas. They were all Air Corps enlistments, mostly from Oklahoma and Iowa.

Private Charles K. Plotner,

"(We) were shipped from Sheppard Field, Texas, to Selfridge Field, Michigan in January of 1942. Sheppard Field had one strand of barbed wire between it and the North Pole and a normal breeze was a thirty mile per hour wind, so we thought that was cold. Then we arrive in Michigan to be greeted by more cold, higher humidity and six to eight inches of snow in the ground.

"Getting off the troop train we were ushered into one of the temporary barracks, up to the second floor no less—and more cold. The next morning after roll call in the snow, we marched over to the permanent barracks for a hot breakfast. Great! Then back into the cold to Supply for an issue of four buckle overshoes and those heavy Army overcoats made of sixty-five ounce wool. This was the garb in which we were introduced to basic training—along with the snow, cold, and wind from the Great Lakes."

First Assignment, Los Angeles, California

Mission: Responsibility for operation of Air/Ground radio stations serving fighter aircraft assigned to Los Angeles, California Air Defense Wing

After a period of organization and training at Selfridge, the unit was ordered to follow their parent organization, the *First Pursuit Group*, headquartered at the Los Angeles Air Defense Wing, departing 11 February 1942. This permanent change of station for the fledgling unit was to March Field, Riverside, California. They arrived by troop train on 15 February 1942, reported to the 4th Interceptor Command, and immediately proceeded by truck to Los Angeles, reporting to the Commanding Officer, Los Angeles Air Defense Wing for temporary duty on 16 February 1942.

On this date the one officer and fifty one enlisted men were re-designated the *1st Fighter Control Squadron (Sep)*.

On 1 March, the new CO, Captain Bolick, began building and training the organization into its unique new mission. On 10 March 1942 twenty eight men were enrolled in Radio Mechanics School at Camp Haan, California. The remainder of the squadron began training in administration, supply, mess, and transportation (at one point the squadron had sixty vehicles.)

Upon the return of the Radio School graduates on 1 May, the unit was assigned the duty to establish an air-to-ground communications system between the fighter aircraft squadrons located in the vicinity of

7

Los Angeles and the control room of the Los Angeles Air Defense Wing.

At this time high frequency (HF) radio was used for the mission. Due to the inadequacy of fighter plane radio equipment at the time, it required many ground stations to maintain proper communications with flights. Ultimately, soldiers of the 1st Fighter Control Squadron were manning and maintaining twelve stations extending from Santa Maria to San Diego, California.

January 1943—installation of Very High Frequency (VHF) radio equipment was initiated, achieving full operation on 30 May 1943. (The HF system also remained in operation as many of the area aircraft were not yet equipped for VHF.) In addition to providing air-to-ground communications, the unit operated one Homing Station and three Directional Finding Radio Stations. The information transmitted from these stations to the control room was vital to providing accurate and constant fighter control.

March 1943—the squadron is reorganized once again under a TO&E calling for twenty four officers and three hundred and twenty three enlisted men.

1 August 1943—Orders increased the strength of the 1st Fighters to thirty four officers and three hundred and thirty nine enlisted men—and re-designated them as the *1st Fighter Control Squadron Special.*

5 August 1943—The 1st Fighter Control Squadron (Special) was alerted for overseas assignment. The commanding officer, Captain Bolick, since promoted to Major, was relieved by Captain Rhinehart H. Miller.

10 August 1943—the unit is relieved from Los Angeles Fighter Wing, replaced by the 37th Fighter Control Squadron who assumed all of the 1st Fighter's equipment, and they moved to March Field for resupply and new equipment.

West Coast Memories of 1st Fighters

Private Charles K. Plotner,

"At Riverside we detrained and loaded onto Army transport trucks to be taken to downtown Los Angeles—8th & Flower. This was an 8 story building which was to be our new barracks. We ate on the 8th floor, slept on the 6th floor, and worked on the 4th floor.

"We were some of the earlier GI arrivals in Los Angeles and enjoyed a few weeks before crowds of servicemen saturated the area. We could get together .50 cents to go to Mike Lyman's bar downtown—about 6 blocks—order a beer and sip away on it until someone offered to buy us dinner or show us around the city.

"We enjoyed many privileges at that time—exercise and swimming at the Elks Lodge on Wilshire Boulevard, tripe to the

Hollywood Canteen where we rubbed elbows with the celebrities and stars, as well as afternoons at the Beverly Hills Hotel where we were photographed with Veronica Lake. This photo was later published in two of the popular movie magazines of those days."

1st Fighter soldiers recall their time in Los Angeles,

"I can remember when we were stationed at 8th and Flower (Streets), downtown Los Angeles. At that time they had the 'zoot suiters.' These were young fellows who wore long, baggy pants with long watch chains hanging almost to their shoes. They usually carried knives and went in gangs of two or more."

"One night, another guy from our squadron and myself were walking down a street in L.A. when from the other side came a gang of those fellows, maybe eight or ten. We knew they all had knives and were looking for trouble, so we hightailed it out of there! We didn't feel like getting all cut up as we were outnumbered. All us servicemen were warned to be on the lookout for those gangs."

"Now how about the *red alert* on the West Coast, called by the San Francisco Air Defense Wing based on reports of unidentified aircraft flying toward the City from the Pacific. When the controller sent a flight in the direction of the incoming radar reports, they found a bunch of pelicans headed determinedly toward the City."

Headed for War

War Department Movement Order 0445, dated 22 August 1943 was received, designating the unit 04450D and setting the readiness date for personnel and organizational equipment for 1 October 1943 (later postponed to 23 October due to an initial scarcity of cryptographic and high speed radio operators).

Captain Irwin C. McBride took command of the unit from Captain Miller and the call of the Port Commander was received 5 October 1943.

Loading of equipment required two boxcars and four flatcars and was completed by 19 October. On 23 October the unit boarded the train for movement to Camp Stoneman, California, and on 27 October they embarked on SS Cape San Juan, sailing on the morning of 28 October 1943. Sergeant Driest noted, "The spirit and morale of the officers and men were high."

Troops on the bow of SS Cape San Juan as it approaches the Golden Gate Bridge near San Francisco. 1943

Chapter Two

A History of Aircraft Interception Early Warning Systems

The US Army Air Corp Fighter Control Squadrons have their roots in the systems developed by the British to defend the island from the German air assaults.

Chester Driest noted, "The basic idea was adapted from the British ... and we even borrowed much of their terminology."

In England the air defense control centers remained fixed in locations along the coast, warning of incoming German attack aircraft and guiding the RAF to intercept points, while the American units like the 1st Fighter Control Squadron in the South Pacific were transported by ship, landed on beachheads and fought their way off the beaches. At the same time they established control centers as quickly as possible after the initial battle, defending the area against Japanese air attacks by guiding American fighter planes to intercept incoming enemy planes. They also provided "homing" communications for lost American pilots, and guidance for air-sea rescue of downed pilots.

British Application/Development of Early Radar Technology

The concept known as GCI—Ground Control Interception—originated with the British. It is an air defense tactic using one or more radar or other observational stations linked to a command communications center which guides friendly interceptor aircraft to an incoming enemy airborne target. This tactic was pioneered during WWII by the RAF (Royal air Force) with the German Luftwaffe to follow closely. Today, GCI is still important, although AWACS (Airborne Early Warning and Control), with or without support from GCI, offers much greater range and accuracy.

Today the term GCI refers to the style of battle direction, but during WWII it included the radars themselves. Specifically, the term was used to describe a new generation of radars that spun on their vertical axis in order to provide a complete 360 degree view of the sky around the station. Previous systems, notably the British *Chain Home* (CH), could only be directed along angles in "front" of the antennas and were unable to direct air traffic once it passed behind their shore-side locations. GCI radars began to replace CH starting in 1941/42, allowing a single station to control the entire battle from early detection to directing the fighters to intercept. Because the Chain Home radar stations faced out to sea, once airborne intruders had crossed the British coast they could no longer be tracked by radar; and accordingly the interception direction centers relied on visual and aural sightings of the Observer Corps for continually updated information on the location and heading of enemy aircraft formations. While this arrangement worked acceptably during the daylight raids of the *Battle of Britain*, subsequent bombing attacks of *The Blitz* demonstrated that such techniques were wholly inadequate for identifying and tracking aircraft at night.

British WWII Antenna array

WWII British underground control room.

Experiments in addressing this problem started with manually directed radars being used as a sort of radio-searchlight, but this proved too difficult to use in practice. Another attempt was made by using a height finding radar turned on its side in order to scan an arc in front of the station. This proved very workable and was soon extended to covering a full 360 degrees by making minor changes to the support and bearing systems. Making a display system, the "Plan Position Indicator" (PPI), that displayed a 360 degree pattern proved surprisingly easy and test systems were available by late 1940. Starting in 1941 the RAF began deploying production models of the GCI radar, first with expedient solutions, and then permanent stations.

As the system became operational the success of the RAF night fighter force began to shoot up and interception rates doubled every month from January 1941 until the *Luftwaffe* campaign ended in May.

The Germans were quite slow to follow in terms of PPI and did not order operational versions of their *Jagdschloss radar* until late in 1943, with deliveries being relatively slow after that. Many were still under construction when the war ended in 1945.

US Radar Application in WWII South Pacific Island Invasions

The American system used TOP SECRET radio equipment such as: point-to-point communications, both long and short range, air-to-ground and ground-to-air, intercept, IFF, FM, HF, Homing Stations,

Radar, Cryptographic equipment, Teletype, and more. Many of the members of the 1st Fighter Control Squadron did not know they had knowledge of and used a system that was one of the best kept secrets of the War. Neither Germans nor the Japanese ever learned or understood why we were so successful in detecting aircraft, giving early warnings, and intercepting their aircraft both during the day and especially at night with the P-61 Black Widow Night Fighter Aircraft.

The United States' development of the smaller, more powerful and portable radars allowed the formation of the "Fighter Control Squadron" units that proved invaluable in the Pacific campaign. With all personnel and equipment coming ashore with the invasion, a "Control Center" operated by the Fighter Control Squadron was quickly established within a few hours H-Hour/D-Day. The Center consisted of a large plotting board on which airmen moved "trees" festooned with cards indicating the size of the enemy and allied flights being tracked with altitude, speed and course being noted. Unidentified aircraft were labelled "bogies," enemy aircraft "bandits," and Allied aircraft ad "friendlies." The men at the plotting boards were connected by radio to outlying radar stations operated by the US Army Signal Corps and similar stations aboard US Navy Destroyers, transferring the information they received to the "trees" on the operations boards.

On a platform above the board a team of Fighter Control Squadron officers, headed by the Air Controller, had the responsibility to call *Red Alerts* when an approaching flight was designates an enemy. The Red Alert meant that all lights in the landing area had to be doused, which reduced any activities to only those that could be done in the dark. It was a delicate balance of decisions. Sergeant Driest wrote, "A false alarm slowed up our attacking forces, but if an area controller failed to call an alert when approaching aircraft were actually the enemy, it exposed our forces to unwarranted danger."

Operations Board in use on Wakde Island (above)
Mindoro, Philippine Islands (below)

Mindoro, Philippines

Standing at the Plotting table inside the 42nd Fighter Control Center.
Clyde M. Eitenhefer, Charles M. Hankins, Benjamin E. Fischer

Chapter Three

Disaster at Sea:
First Taste of Battle and Casualties

The Cover Art for the Novel Featuring the Experiences
of 1ˢᵗ Fighter Control Squadron

It was early morning, 0530 local time, on 11 November 1943 and *SS Cape San Juan* was steaming on a westerly course at 14.7 knots per hour, about three hundred miles southeast of Fiji. The weather was clear and the seas slightly choppy with a few whitecaps. The sun had not yet risen, but it was light enough to see clearly.

The 2ⁿᵈ Mate, William J. Dorcey was on watch and the ship's Master, Walter M. Strong, was on the bridge standing just to the port side of the binnacle stand. Most of the one thousand four hundred and sixty four men on board were still in their bunks, although breakfast in #2 Hold was just beginning to be served.

The American troopship, *SS Cape San Juan*, was on her second voyage, sailing unescorted from San Francisco to Townsville, Australia. She had fifty-seven Merchant Crew, forty-two Navy Armed Guards, and three radio operators, and was transporting three US Army Air Corp units to the Pacific War Theater:

855th Engineer (Aviation) Bn, "All Negro"—811 men
The 253rd Ordnance (Aviation) Company—162 men
The 1st Fighter Control Squadron—367 men

There were also twenty-one "permanent" army personnel, commanded by Major Robert A. Barth, who were responsible for the troops while being transported, plus one unidentified civilian.

Total: 1,464 men.

SS Cape San Juan was blacked out, zigzagging, and had lookouts posted with the Navy Armed Guard crew at general quarters. As she was executing a turn to starboard in accordance with her zig-zag plan, torpedo tracks were spotted by lookouts. Within seconds she was hit by a torpedo fired by the Japanese Imperial Navy I-21 submarine commanded by Commander Hiroshi Inada.

The account of that day that follows represents the greatest loss of life of any American-Hawaiian Steamship operated vessel. While no Merchant Mariner or Armed Guard were among the casualties, the loss of life among her US military passengers was significant. But as significant as that loss was, the fact that over a thousand men entered the oily, shark infested, fifteen foot rain-swept seas that November morning in the South Pacific, and all but 117 made it out, is nothing short of a miracle. A miracle created by men selflessly putting their own lives at risk to help others—from ship and aircraft crews to the soldiers themselves in the cold water, encouraging their buddies and total strangers to "hold on just a little longer."

Various eyewitness accounts described the morning:

"Two water spouts seen at a distance of approximately 2000 yards; relative bearing 120 degrees. Wake seen on water when 15 yards distant from the ship; very straight path; approximately 2 feet wide; went aft of vessel, missing stern by 20 yards. Wake was light greenish color; water itself was deep dark green. Left slight white foam on surface."

Another eyewitness claims he saw the wake of this torpedo some 300 feet out on the starboard quarter and claims that it missed the ship's stern by only 15 feet. A few seconds after first torpedo passed aft of vessel several armed guard lookouts saw two water spouts, generally described as from 6 to 10 feet high and from 2 to 3 feet in width. Both spouts broke the surface at a distance of from 1500 to 2500 yards, relative bearing 130 degrees. They were described as egg-shaped by one witness, as fan shaped by another, and as being "in the shape of a pine tree" by another.

"When some 250 yards from ship, this wake broke and an object skimmed on the surface of the water, in the line of the wake, for a distance of some 20 feet. It traveled so fast that no one could identify color, shape or size. When object submerged, wake did not reappear and explosion against starboard side of ship immediately followed. Torpedo struck starboard, abreast of the after end of No. 2 hatch, far below water line."

Because of the quantity of oil which emerged to the surface immediately after torpedo hit, it is believed to have struck very close to the double bottom. A heavy oil slick immediately appeared. Inasmuch as the ship immediately took on a hard starboard list, the exact position, size, shape of hole and damage done to the hull could not be viewed or ascertained.

When the torpedo struck, eye witnesses stated that,

> "Immediately on the impact, a great flash of light came up over the gunwale on the starboard quarter, reaching as high as the ship's bridge and covering a width of over 20 feet." They went on to describe the color of the explosion, the smoke that immediately followed, and finally the water that cascaded back down onto the vessel."

> They described the impact, "The ship shook and shuddered and the bow raised slightly, then settled and the vessel took on an immediate 10 degree to 15 degree list to starboard, and then settled to a 20 degree to 25 degree list within a few minutes."

The torpedo struck below where the troops from the 855th were berthed—the #2 Hold. The hatch covers over the hold were blown upwards, and then collapsed down into the void, killing and injuring several men. An *SOS* was sent along with the message, *"Torpedoed, ship sinking fast."*

Inexplicably, the Officer in Charge of the radio, Lt. (j.g.) Harris, ordered the radio destroyed immediately afterwards and then he abandoned ship, so no further signals were sent. Some effort was made to repair the equipment, but to no avail.

The Navy Armed Guard returned fire immediately towards the area the submarine was believed to have fired from. All guns fired intermittently for about ten minutes. Occasional shots were fired throughout the day to let the enemy know they were still aboard.

The ship's engine were ordered stopped and she coasted to a stop as she continued her turn to starboard. The evacuation, mainly of the enlisted Army personnel, commenced about fifteen to twenty minutes after being hit. More torpedoes were expected at any moment. The seas started to deteriorate into fifteen foot seas with white caps. The #2 Hold flooded quickly and the ship settled down by the bow with the starboard list increasing.

It is unclear exactly how many men perished from the initial torpedo explosion, subsequent flooding, and the collapse of the hatch structure. Some men drowned during *abandon ship* by jumping over board in full combat gear, and others were lost who were in the water near the ship when large wooden rafts were released over them.

Understandably, most men in the water, and even in the rafts, tried to get to the few life boats, which soon became heavily overloaded. The #4 motorboat was swamped and lost when too many men, estimated at sixty-five, attempted to board it. Another came very close to capsizing. Some rafts drifted away before they could be manned, described as "*not less than two and not more than six.*"

Many of the men initially ended up with nothing but a life vest. These were a mix of cork and kapok and years later, survivors Chester Driest and James Reed would laugh at how some of the life vests were stenciled *For Inland Waterways Only*.

Wind and wave action quickly dispersed the men in the water to the south and the oil caused severe eye irritation and even temporary blindness in some cases.

The apparent gash along the port stern is an illusion. It is a result of burned paint and the angle of the light.
(Ed. Note: The Navy's designation, USAT, is United State Army Transport. The common designation is SS - Steam Ship)

A photo from a Royal New Zealand Air Force aircraft. The small rescue vessel at left is probably the mine sweeper YMS-241.

The first rescue ship on the scene that day was the Liberty Ship Edwin T. Meredith, commanded by Murdock D. McRae. She arrived five and a half hours after the torpedoing.

After transferring the casualties and excess survivors still on board SS Cape San Juan, Meredith circled the ship for eight hours, picking up survivors in the water. Several of her Merchant Seamen and Navy Armed Guard crew exhibited extreme courage by diving into the heavy, shark infested, oil covered sea to pull exhausted men to the side of the ship where they could be hauled up to safety.

Chief Mate Al Appelbaum of the Edwin T. Meredith, described the scene of horror he found when his ship reached the scene of the torpedoing,

"Sharks tore bodies from partially submerged life rafts in their hunger for human flesh. Some of the sharks had already made off with screaming men, and the blood from the bodies of those boys attracted more sharks. There were schools of them, I don't know how many, but they were seven to ten feet long— they even pulled men off rafts."

The Meredith's captain asked for volunteers to man a motor lifeboat and go over to Cape San Juan.

Chief Mate Appelbaum reports,

"It was raining and there were heavy seas. First Engineer Maurey Scott of Venice, California, went with me as engineer in a motor lifeboat, and we had three sailors."

25

"I pulled alongside (Cape San Juan) and asked Captain Strong for instructions. He asked that we first take stretcher cases off immediately—men wounded by the torpedo hit."

More small boats went into the water to aid in the rescue. Chief Appelbaum continued,

"All this time the water was infested with men on rafts, men clinging to wreckage, and men just swimming. The sharks were already there. Some of the rafts were partly submerged, and I saw men actually pulled off by the sharks."

"On one of the trips over I saw an Army captain going down and a shark circling around him. I dove overboard and got the captain into our boat. We got him aboard ship and he had a pint of whiskey on him. We didn't have a drop of whiskey on the ship, but this captain would not share a drink with us— said he was saving it."

The merchant seamen continued rescue operations until some of them dropped from sheer exhaustion. They won the unreserved praise of those who were there.

Eighteen-year-old Donald Peter Adams, one of the Navy men cited for bravery in rescuing a man from drowning in the shark-infested waters, brushed off his experience with, "I just went down into the water, grabbed him, and helped him aboard—that's all."

Other vessels that responded to the rescue call were the destroyer USS McCalla, DD-488, the mine sweeper YMS-241, and the submarine chaser SC-654. The heroic actions of the crews of these vessels in the rescue operation is documented elsewhere.

USS McCalla - DD-488. Photo courtesy of navsource.org.

USS McCalla DD-488

No known pictures exist of SC-654 or SC-1043, but these small wooden vessels, the smallest commissioned warships in the US fleet all belong to the same class 497 in WWII and were very similar in design and layout. This is an example of SC663. They were quite a bit smaller than even the YMS-241 at 98; 116ft 10in long. Armament: 1 40mm gun mount, 1 or 2 twin mount .50 cal. machine guns, 2 or 3 "K Guns", 14 depth charges with 6 single release chocks, 2 sets Mk 20 Mousetrap rails with 4 7.2 projectiles. Complement: 3 officers, 24 enlisted. Speed: 21 kts. Simply amazing that SC-654 was able to pick up 152 survivors in 10+ foot seas. National Archives Photo RG-19-LCM circa May 1945 courtesy of www.navsource.org.

SC 654 has no known photographs. Above is a similar vessel.

27

PROGRESS PHOTOS
YMS 241

Hull No. 44
View Three Quarter Bow

TACOMA BOAT BUILDING CO.
Tacoma, Washington

Hoyer & Co.
20 Feb 1943   Photo

USN Minesweeper YMS-241 underway. The small 320t, 136ft long wooden hulled vessel was original designed from inshore mine sweeping. Armament: 1 3"/50, 2 20mm, & 2 depth charge projectors. Complement: 4 Officers, 29 Crew. Speed: 13knts. Photo courtesy of Dr. Tom Gauthier.

Minesweeper YMS-241

Vessel of same type as Liberty Ship Edwin T. Meredith

Rescue from the Air

There was another response to the SOS of SS Cape San Juan, unusual and dramatic. The next rescue vessel on the scene was not a ship, but an unarmed Pan American Martin Mariner, PBM-3R, flying boat, piloted by Captain William W. Moss, Jr.

His crew aboard included First Officer Frank W. Saul, Second Officer George H. Robin, Engineer Officer Harry L. Knebel, Radio Officer Don V. Mackay, and Steward Kenneth S. Taylor, all volunteers. They were Naval Air Transport Service Flight V2163, now on a mercy mission.

The aircraft had just arrived in Fiji that morning on their way to Noumea from Pearl Harbor when word of the sinking was announced. Bill Moss, his crew, and Navy Pharmacist Mate A. Burress from the Navy base, volunteered to search for survivors.

Moss noted in his report that Third Officer J. B. Kelly, Assistant Engineering Officer A. F. Aready, and Assistant Radio Officer D. Holton also volunteered but were left behind to make room for more survivors.

As they were preparing to leave, a Navy Captain who had been a passenger aboard the PBM from Pearl approached Moss and asked to come along, which Moss had to refuse. The unidentified Captain handed him five bottles of I.W. Harper, top-shelf Kentucky

Straight Bourbon Whiskey which he was bringing to Admiral Halsey and said, "If you need it, use it."

Moss handed the whiskey to his steward, Kenny Taylor.

The original plan for the mission called for landing at the scene of the disaster, picking up as many survivors as was considered possible, taking off, and proceeding to Tonga Tabu, discharging passengers and returning to the scene to repeat the procedure. After unloading their cargo they topped off all their fuel tanks, and loaded rafts, life vests and extra line, and took off at 1239.

At 1244 they were ordered to abort the mission, but they radioed back requesting permission to continue, which was granted at 1249.

About halfway through the flight they ran into a tropical storm. What they found as they came out of the storm clouds was the SS Cape San Juan still afloat about 10 miles dead ahead.

At first they only saw the life boats and rafts. Then they noticed small clusters of black dots, which they soon realized were men wearing life vests. The swells were described as "confused" with the wind at ten to twelve knots, and Moss had a difficult time finding a patch smooth enough to attempt a landing.

These planes were designed to take off from sheltered bays, not the open ocean, and especially the ocean under these conditions.

The large amount of oil in the water smoothed out the waves somewhat in the immediate vicinity, so Moss set up his approach for the smoothest spot he could find. He attempted to land crosswind, opting to try and maintain relative motion with the swell as best he could. Everything was looking good as he came in at seventy knots until he hit the first wave crest which slammed the plane fifty feet back into the air. Moss dumped the throttles and held the elevators full back as the nose hit successive sides of waves in an extremely violent manner. As a matter of fact, so violent were the shocks that Moss did not believe the plane would remain in a floatable condition, let alone be flyable. After a quick inspection verified they were okay, they began formulating a plan to rescue the men in the sea.

They decided to concentrate on the most vulnerable men, those not in rafts. It was deemed too risky to try and maneuver the plane through the men, and the survivors were too exhausted to swim for the plane. So they devised a system where they trolled for survivors by towing a string of small rafts behind them as they zig-zagged upwind along the edge of the rescue area.

Moss stayed at the controls, blipping the throttle continually to steer the plane while the rest of the crew were aft, reeling the survivors in and lifting them into the plane. Several of the crew were incapacitated by seasickness as the plane rolled in the heavy swells.

Forty-eight soldiers were rescued in this manner, roughly split 50/50 between black troops and white troops. Their oily, water soaked clothes were stripped off and thrown back into the sea, and they were given blankets, food, hot coffee, water—and a shot of the Admiral's whiskey.

Black and white image of a watercolor pointing of the rescue plane by combat artist Lieutenant Seymour Thompson, USNR. The image was included in a Collier's Magazine article about the rescue in October 1944.

A Royal New Zealand Air Force Hudson Bomber was circling the scene. After two hours of this grueling work the American PBM crew saw it fire two red flares in their direction. The two planes were not able to communicate via radio, and Moss assumed the signal meant danger (possibly the submarine surfacing for attack).

Knowing his crew was exhausted, his plane at maximum capacity, and with another heavy rain squall closing in, Moss made the difficult decision to quit while they were ahead.

Since it had taken much longer than expected to collect survivors, Moss knew he didn't have time to reach Tonga Tabu, unload, and get back to the stricken ship before nightfall. He therefore dropped both auxiliary fuel tanks to lighten the load. As it was, he estimated his gross takeoff weight at 45,258 pounds.

The difficult take-off was achieved in only about fifty seconds, but what a ride. They had to make the attempt downwind since the squall was closing from the right and survivors blocked the other side.

According to Moss,

"At 55 knots the plane bounced off the top of a wave to a height of 30 to 50 feet, setting up a series of five or six bounces until the plane finally became airborne at approximately 70-75 knots. On the second bounce the left wing dropped approximately twenty degrees, but full aileron control brought it up before the plane touched the water again."

It took an exceedingly long time before the plane was able to increase its speed and altitude. The takeoff was considered by the crew to be much more violent than the landing.

Many years later Frank Saul would describe it as, "The hairiest take-off of my life."

Moss simply stated, "It was the longest 50 seconds of my life."

An Eye Witness Description of the Takeoff

Extract from a report by the crew of the Royal New Zealand Air Force Hudson bomber that had circled the scene to protect from Japanese submarines.

"At briefing we learned that the San Juan, carrying some 1,429 service personnel, was torpedoed at 0900 hours. F/O Stan Kirk of Auckland replaced our Navigator, P/O Ross Laurenson, Seatoun, Wellington—a welcome break for Ross as he was really tired.

"We were airborne by 1250 hours and arrived in the area at 1620 hours, it being covered by a tropical rain storm. There was only one approach and that was a low level run at 70 feet. We leveled out and even then visibility was poor, but any lower was dangerous as we could have run into the stricken ship.

"We had covered about four miles when suddenly there was a clear patch in the weather. What a sight unfolded before us! Hundreds of men in the sea below us and many, many more crammed onto bits of timber, life rafts, Carley floats, duck boards, and pitifully few life boats.

"Off to the left, and right on the edge of the rain, was a liberty ship (*Ed. Note: SS Edwin T. Meredith*) with landing nets or cargo nets over the side. The captain of the ship was steaming very slowly through the survivors. Many were able to climb up the nets to safety;

however, he did not stop for fear of being torpedoed himself. When he cleared the rain squall - full steam for Noumea, we spotted a few seconds later the Martin Mariner, a Pan American Airways flying boat, but were unable to make radio contact with her.

"We estimated a sixteen foot swell was running. It had picked up some forty-plus men and was not happy about taking off, as he had damaged his starboard float. We continued flying around in a tight sweep, flying very low; some survivors waved to us, and others I sadly noted were floating face down in their life jackets. Harry Farmiloe's came through the intercom system, 'Stand by, the PBM is going to attempt to take off.' We all offered a prayer for any wounded and the passengers in that aircraft as we knew full well what they would go through in the next two to three minutes.

"The Mariner turned into the wind, looking like a massive bird with her gull wing and twin tail. I became alarmed that she was riding too low in the water. I racked my brains on aircraft recce—yes, she had a carrying capacity of only about three tons, with forty-plus men on, that's at least an extra 1 1/2 tons!

"She was now riding the swell and gaining speed into the wind, leaving a white trail of foam behind her. Suddenly she altered course to port, thus giving a little more lift to the damaged float on the starboard wing. At this point she started to go through the tops of the swells, the tips of her propellers striking the sea, sending up great clouds of spray. The revs of the motors would drop rapidly, then as she went into the trough she would build up to full revs again, repeating the performance again and again, until sufficient speed and wind built up under the wings to give her lift, then she started hitting the tops of the swell with a mighty thump, leaving a trail of evenly-spaced white patches of foam behind her. Suddenly they ceased and, thank God, she was airborne.

Drawing by the American PBM's Second Officer George H. Robin, made during flight after the rescue of Cape San Juan survivors

Personal Memories of 1st Fighters

Technical Sergeant Mitchell "Red" Williamson,

"Our patch of the Pacific was dark and stormy at 0530 on November 11, 1943. Just another day of WWII aboard the troop transport Cape San Juan as it plowed a huge phosphorescent furrow 300 miles off the Fiji Islands. The enlisted men were asleep in canvas-bottom, hammock-style bunks amid the snores and foul air of the lower deck in Hatch One.

"Suddenly there was a terrific raring impact and a geyser of spray and debris just aft of Hatch Two. I was catapulted onto the steel deck two bunks below mine. A shower of PX snacks, canteen belts and GI shoes pelted me soundly before I got to my feet, bruised and bordering on panic. On all sides around me, other rudely awakened Joes picked themselves up gingerly, hardly believing they were still in one piece. "Then came the babble of pandemonium as we grabbed helmets and rushed for the stairs. Some men dressed in everything, including leggings.

"We quickly discovered that our hatch door was locked topside. Too many wounded in the way, someone said—and the deck was all torn up. Word came down to send up any medics—the rest of us were to stay below for now., Few of us questioned that we had been hit by a Jap torpedo, as our deck guns were booming away. We didn't know whether the sub had surfaced or what. The order to *abandon ship* came over the PA, and most of the surviving troops topside had gone.

"I saw Nichols, a long, tall drink-of-water, saying goodbye to his buddies. Several men were praying aloud. Almost all had their shoes on by now, and their OD's. A Merchant seaman had told us to wear dark fatigues instead of suntans if we ever had to leave the ship because it was more difficult for sharks to spot us. Finally the line began to move topside, and it was like being released from a tomb. Nearly out, I felt a strong urge to go back down for my pocket copy of the New Testament. My buddies might say it was a sudden case of religion, or an attempt to use Scripture as a talisman, but I took time to fetch it anyway—and felt better for it.

"On deck, the first rays of dawn starkly revealed a grisly scene. In Hatch Two, occupied by the black aviation engineer troops, each deck level had collapsed from top to bottom. Most of the instantaneous deaths and critical injuries had happened there. One look into that gory, moaning mass of humanity made me sick. Biting away the nausea, I asked an officer if I could help.

"He said, 'No more needed below, but the gun crew made a call for ammo passers.' I pressed through the crowd in that direction, but before I could make it to the guns they had their quota. I would only be in the way.

"From all sides, officers were waving their arms and shouting at the remaining troops to abandon ship immediately. There was just one problem—all the life boats and rafts were out there in turbulent waves, already so overloaded they seemed to be submerged.

"Here at last was something for me to do. I joined a group of men frantically throwing overboard every floatable object—wooden kegs, empty fuel tins, planks, and hatch covers. The supply was soon exhausted, and the officers became more insistent that we abandon the ship. One lieutenant was leaning over the ship's rail firing his revolver over the heads of a few men who were blocking traffic at the foot of the rope-net ladder. They were too scared to drop off into the water and too weak to climb back up.

"I understood their reluctance—the San Juan was still afloat high above the seething waves and compared to the plight of the men in the ocean, she seemed like the Rock of Gibraltar—but its severe list made it more like the

39

Leaning Tower of Pisa. I wondered if the shouting officers were still aboard because of heroism or their own fear of the shark-infested water.

"Myers (Private Kenneth M.), a red-faced blond kid of 18, caught my arm in a vise-like grip and said, "Are you going over?" He looked as scared as I felt.

'I suppose so—that's the order.'

He answered, 'But I can't swim a stroke.' He had a faint grin on his face.

'You're in good company,' I told him. 'I can only swim one breath's worth.'

Myers seemed to feel better.

'Well, then. If you'll go over, I will too.'

"I told him he had a deal, and took off my steel outer helmet, keeping the liner as sun protection. I also decided to wear my shoes in spite of their weight.

"Climbing down the rope ladder, I saw the oil—odd I hadn't noticed it before. It covered the water as far as I could see. Two men still clung tenaciously to the ladder below me and I was forced to drop over them from above. The diesel fuel oil covered me instantly and my eyes began to sting fiercely.

"I had lost contact with Myers in the descent, and now my only concern was getting away from the ship as fast as I could. I didn't want to be nearby if another Jap tin fish should strike—and if

that oil caught fire! And what if the sub
crew decided to surface and strafe us. I
didn't even have a pocket knife for
protection against sharks!

"These panicky thoughts seemed
absolutely unreal, even as they raced
through my mind. But it was no dream.
Those waves seemed mountainous now,
flooding over my head as they struck with
drum-roll regularity. The oil and salt
water made a noxious combination to
swallow and I quickly began choking and
vomiting.

"A few wave-tops ahead of me, a
group of men seemed to be on a raft. I
made no headway trying to reach them,
and began to freeze, my legs and feet
cramping. I threw off the helmet liner
because the strap was choking me. Each
time I vomited, I swallowed more oil and
sea water—then retched again. Death
began to seem almost attractive. I had
never felt so helpless.

"A sudden change in the direction of
the waves brought me abruptly into the
midst of eight men on a plank. I could
distinguish black men from white men
only by their voices. The blacks were
praying and singing hymns with what
strength they could muster. I grabbed a
handhold and commenced my own
prayers.

"I was no longer freezing, only
numb, nauseated and thoroughly

wretched. With each crashing wave, the slippery oil-covered plank spun out of our grasp, and we grabbed again. It helped a little when I found a knothole that accommodated one thumb.

"Time floated into space, everything becoming more nightmarish by the minute. I thought of my loved ones, of Bernice and our unborn child. In two weeks I would be a father—and Bernice might be a widow. Just grit my teeth and hold on—no use giving up. But others were—like the black engineer who, unknown to the rest of us, had made his final decision. "God, I can't take this," he said, quickly shoving away from the plank and loosening his life preserver before anyone could stop him. Within ten hours, three more of these men were to be lost.

"At about 1000 we heard planes. And then there they were, two New Zealand Air Force planes. Useless for rescue work, they were still a fantastic boost for morale. We waved crazily, cheering too. Someone knew our position—rescue ships must be on the way. It warmed our hearts to see those planes dip their wings encouragingly. Finally, they merged into the horizon and time glided on, keeping silent vigil with the wind, the waves, and the wails. My eyes were closed now. I was so weak I wondered how I stayed with that slippery plank. Surely my hands had grown to it.

"Then, as the sun peaked overhead, I became vaguely conscious of excited voices that spoke of a ship and rang a gong in my head. My eyelids struggled open and, between the towering waves, I made out the black form of a freighter on the far horizon. Too exhausted to celebrate, I still evaluated my chances of getting to that beautiful silhouette. Out of the question, I decided. We were miles away and drifting swiftly in the opposite direction. More time and tide, interrupted only when one of our cramp-legged group would try to straddle the plank for some relief. The others had to break up such a move with admonishments that sounded more understanding than angry.

"Out of the storm clouds like a silver miracle, a large flying boat suddenly swooped towards the ocean on our right. That pilot I thought, was crazy to try landing on such monstrous waves; but he finally made it. Everyone was wide awake now, and my mind struggled with one critical question. We were almost exactly halfway between the ship and the plane. Which to try? The ship was larger and more substantial---but so had been the Cape San Juan; and our drift was slightly toward the plane. One man wished us luck and took off trying to swim for the plane. Within a half hour, only an engineer and I remained on the plank. He had become increasingly concerned as each man left, and I stayed with him as long as I dared. I tried to reassure him about his rescue chances, but my voice must have sounded hollow and unconvincing. I was trying to bolster my own nerve enough to leave that floating plank.

"The PBM was now just a few hundred yards off; sink or swim, I had to go for it. The black engineer began to moan softly as I left; I've never quite lost the traitorous feeling of that moment. As he had steadfastly refused to leave the plank, I could only tell myself he would be no worse off except for being along.

"The plane's motors were being gunned for the takeoff warmup, and my frantically waving arm would not be seen. Now it was my turn to feel abandoned as the plane started to move, its nose pointing away from me. But abruptly it became an answered prayer, turning with a dramatic sweep for its take off run directly towards me. There could be no weakness now; I waved my arm and yelled desperately, dredging up the strength from deep within. The big silver bird hesitated, then slowed. Two men appeared in the hatchway and hurled a heaving line with a perfect cast. Grabbing the ring at the end, I held on for dear life—literally. The surging swells made the plane bob vigorously in the ocean. It took both men long minutes to reel me alongside and hoist me bodily through the hatchway.

"I lay there, too weak to move, loving the solid floor, and offering silent thanks. Crew members stripped off my heavy, oil-and waterlogged clothing and tossed everything overboard. The fatigues contained my money, watch and a soggy New Testament; but I couldn't speak up quickly enough to say so.

"I was wrapped in a blanket and helped to a spot out of the aisle. Two small but warming jiggers of bourbon were poured down my swollen gullet, and my head throbbed itself to sleep. I later learned the liquor was from Admiral 'Bull' Halsey's private stock."

"Days later in the hospital at Suva, Fiji, I was told that except for a Pharmacist's Mate taken aboard to help with the wounded, the crew of the Martin Mariner and formerly operated it for Pan Am. Both plane and crew went into Navy service after Pearl Harbor. Five hours after the torpedoing, Captain W. W. Moss and his crew landed at Suva with supplies. Learning of our plight, all volunteered to fly into 300 miles of lightning, torrential rain and turbulent winds on the rescue mission. Three of the men and much of the plane' normal gear

45

were left behind to make room for supplies and rescued men.

"When Captain Moss tried to put the plane down, the high seas and gale-like wind quickly coated the windshield with the San Juan's diesel oil. Only after seven unsuccessful attempts, with the plane taking a merciless pounding, did he finally catch a wave crest at precisely the right moment and settle the Mariner into the water.

"The exhausted troops in the rough sea could give no help in their rescue, and two of the plan's own crew became helplessly seasick. But with dogged determination and more than two hours of grueling effort, the fliers finally pulled forty-eight men aboard (twenty from our squadron)—more than twice the PBM's normal capacity.

"The overloaded takeoff was another miracle, Moss feared the hull would split apart as it struck wave crests three times, once almost turning on her side, during his struggle to get airborne. All the way back to Fiji, the battered bird sounded like a GI truck on a rocky road.

"Yet to me it was a glorious ride, as I alternately slept and woke to find myself reviewing those ten terrible hours in the Pacific. As unforgettable scenes flashed before me, I had a sense of an enormous debt I had to pay. The day had held so many times and ways that death could have taken me by the hand. But I knew who actually had; and in the years since my ordeal, I've learned He renders his miraculous services free of charge. The debt was paid in full two thousand years ago.

"One more thing I have come to know. The beautiful twofold meaning of the grand old hymn that says, *Love Lifted Me*."

Chester Driest, Technical Sergeant,

"The ship was taking on water very quickly and beginning to list. The order was given to abandon ship and troops were going over the side into the oil-covered water— which soon caused us internal sickness and severe eye problems."

"This photo (above, YMS-241) is the view that I shall always remember, because it was what I saw after being in the water for thirty-six hours with only my life jacket for support—most of the time alone.

"As this vessel came near me and I looked up at the bow, there stood two U.S. Navy sailors with their rifles shooting into the water—at sharks that were swimming around me. At the same instant, two more sailors dove into the water and swam over to me with a rope. Placing it under my arms, they told me to hang on and others on deck would pull me up. As I was placed on deck, the crew moved aft to make room for me. I sat on the oily deck, resting my back against a full canvas bag to support myself.

As I spread my arms back, leaning into the bag, what I felt gave me a sick feeling. I called to one of the sailors and asked him what was in the bag. He answered, 'Someone not as lucky as you were with the sharks.'

"I learned later from the crew of the mine sweeper that many others were not so fortunate. Sharks were still there through the second day and killed or injured many of our troops. Yes, that is the way it was back in November of 1943."

(Ed. Note: Chester Driest inserted the following log)

Ship's Log

Minesweeper YMS-241, 12 Nov 1943

Steaming as before,

1230 changed speed to 14 knots (132 RPM)
1400 commenced maneuvering to take SC-654 alongside for transfer of survivors. (*Ed. note: SC-654 is a small submarine chaser)*

1425 SC-654 came alongside to starboard for transfer of personnel

1445 received about 152 additional survivors. SC-654 left from alongside to proceed to Tonga Tabu due to lack of fuel. Dempsey and YMS-241 maneuvering to transfer survivors from YMS-241 to Dempsey (ed. Note: USS Dempsey, DE-26, destroyer escort)

1532 transfer completed. Dempsey was unable to take more than about 50 men due to weather.

Private Max L. Putnam,

(Ed. Note: Private Putnam had a very dramatic experience, but related privately that the worst of it as far as he was concerned was, "that first meal I got after reaching Fiji—it was absolutely lousy. What a trial after being rescued!")

"We sailed from San Francisco under the Golden Gate Bridge on 23 Oct. 1943 on the SS Cape San Juan. It was not a luxury ship. Our bunks were so close together we couldn't bend our knees up because they would hit the guy in the bunk above. How could anyone forget the salt water showers, one canteen of water a day, and the biggest treat of all—a bottle of cold Coca Cola in the afternoon? I would find a shady spot and nurse that Coke as long as I could.

"At night during the next two weeks I watched phosphorus boil up like light bulbs in the water behind the props of the ship. I watched flying fish skip from wave to wave, and I remember the sea of doldrums where looked as if the water was as smooth as a mirror. I remember the celebration when we crossed the equator and the ship's crew sprayed us all with sea water to initiate us.

"I always awakened early and was one of the first in the chow line because the food looked better at the beginning than at the end. Also, the mess hall was cleaner and the floor wasn't so slippery. Day in and day out, our routine was the same—calisthenics in the morning, show lines, and a cold Coke in the afternoon.

"On 11 November 1943 I was up on deck waiting for chow and leaning over the rail on the port side of the ship when all of a sudden the ship went out from under me. I spun around to protect myself from going backwards and my knees banged up against the center hold. Both my knees were split open and although I didn't feel any damage to my kneecaps, some blood was running down my shins.

"A Japanese torpedo had struck the ship opposite to where I was standing. It wasn't long before men started coming out of the hold. One of the first was our captain. He had his helmet on backwards and was trying to take command of the situation. We had a lot of previous instructions about keeping our life jackets with us at all times, and to listen to instructions from the ship's captain. Also, we were told not to abandon ship unless we were ordered to.

"I watched as our captain ran to the large rafts made of 60 gallon drums and planking. They were on sloping racks at the edge of the ship and held in place with a chain, a lever, and a ring. A marlin tie held the ring in place. You had to cut this tie and slide the ring back, and this released the chain so the raft would release. Our captain was cutting the rafts loose and the ship was still coasting. I know we lost 4 or 5 big rafts because of that.

"Art Altuna came out of the hold and we decided to try to stick together. It seemed like chaos ruled the ship. Some of the big hold beams had come out of their slots and fallen down into the hold. This exposed the ventilating hatch covers that were made out of wood with slots. The overall size of these cover was about 2 by 4 feet. I knew we had already lost some of our rafts, so Altuna and I threw most of the hatch covers overboard from the center hold. A lot of soldiers had abandoned ship and as soon as we threw the hatch covers over, they were grabbed by guys in the water.

"Finally, we were told to abandon ship and people were jumping off as fast as they could. Altuna and I looked over the side, and frothing oil was all around. We decided the best thing to do was to climb down a rope and ease into the oil—if it got into our eyes it would probably blind us. We threw a couple of hatch covers over for ourselves, but by the time we went down the rope they were gone. Remember, our kapok life preservers were stamped with 'Good for 72 Hours,' so Altuna and I looked for something that would last longer. We swam to an inflatable raft which was so heavily loaded that it was under water, and we held onto the rope that goes around the edge. I remember that my shoes seemed heavy, but I thought of my white feet and how they might look like fish bait so decided to leave them on.

"We were still in the oil and there were blankets all around saturated with it. We pushed them away again and again, but they always drifted back. Altuna and I fought them quite a while, and all of a sudden it felt like we were in a Jacuzzi. Bubbles were coming up all around us. It hit me we might be in the wake of another torpedo and I knew if it hit the ship it could hurt my abdomen so I floated on my back—if there was an explosion I wouldn't feel the concussion so much. Nothing happened, so I figured it missed the ship or it was too deep because the ship was listing.

"It wasn't long after when some bombers flew over with their bomb bays wide open. I wondered if they spotted the sub, would they drop bombs on it, and hoped they wouldn't spot the sub. I realized that at least the Army knew our location and we could be rescued.

"Soon after the bombers left a big storm came up and waves rose to a height of 15 to 20 feet. A few hours later while the storm was still raging, an amphibious plane finally landed in the waves after many attempts. It was able to rescue only 49 of the survivors.

"Because of the heavy storm we couldn't see the men around us. The raft we were hanging onto was going up and down like a yoyo. One moment we would be in a hole of water 20 or more feet deep and the next up on top with white cresting waves all around us. Later that day we could see a ship in the distance, and it just sat in the water waiting for survivors to drift to it. It was a long distance from our raft, and before sunset it steamed away.

"All night long we saw nothing. The men on the raft were pretty good. The center was filled with men kneeling down while others sat on the edge with their feet inside. Altuna and I were hanging onto ropes on the outside of the raft. One guy kept throwing up on the men in the middle and someone said, 'Turn your head and throw up outside the raft.' The sick soldier was crying and said that he was too scared to turn his head. One of the men in the center kneeling down was from Switzerland and he kept saying in a strong accent, 'Be braff boys, be braff boys.' Altuna was a Catholic and he kept saying his rosary. Every so often, one of the men in the raft would say, 'It's time for another prayer.'

"I was the only L.D.S. member in the squadron who would admit to being a Mormon. The hymn, *Come Ye Saints*, kept going through my head. One of the lines goes, 'And should we die before our journeys through, Happy Day! All is well!' My forefathers sang that song when they crossed the plains in 1847, after Governor Boggs of Illinois issued an order to exterminate the Mormons. I always associated that song with courage, and I needed all I could get at the time. In all the time in the water, I never felt panic-stricken or desperate and for that I'm truly grateful.

"The storm continued and the day stretched out. We had no water or food. I figured it had been 36 hours or more since we were torpedoed. A lot of the guys seemed to lose hope of the rescue. Late that day we saw another ship south of us that looked like a navy vessel. We thought it wouldn't run away from a submarine. It looked like a destroyer and our hopes went up because we thought the ship would fight rather than run. We continued our slow drift toward it, and the storm raged on. The ship couldn't launch any small craft because of the storm so we had to drift toward it, and after hours and hours we were close enough to swim for it. It was nearly dark, but we could see seamen with rifles on the deck. It looked like they were ready to shoot at sharks around the ship. Altuna and I left the raft and swam toward it. There was a Jacobs' ladder over the side, but the ship was rolling so much the deck was down to water level then up 10 to 12 feet in seconds. When we got close I remembered all of that steel going up and down and knew we had to get close enough to grab onto the ladder. I waited until the ship rolled down and grabbed for the top of the ladder. I thought I could scramble up as easy as pie, but my legs didn't function. Two seamen grabbed my arms and pulled me up on deck. My legs were rubbery and I had to walk around to get the feeling back in them. I stripped off my fatigues and a seaman gave me a pair of underwear shorts to put on.

"A lot of stories circulated through the survivors. One of them was that one of our men kept yelling we would never be rescued, took off his life jacket and gave up. When they pulled the Swiss boy up on deck his legs locked and he couldn't straighten them. I remember the seamen carrying him off the deck with his legs locked up and he was screaming in pain. I wonder how long it took to get his legs stretched out.

"One gruesome story was that a G.I. got close to the ship but his head was hanging down like he had passed out. A seaman jumped into the water to rescue him, but his stomach was gone and all that remained was a cavity. The seaman took off the man's life jacket and dog tags and let the body sink into the water.

"Sometimes I reflect on things that could have been done to help the men in the water, but most of them had grit and that is why so many survived. Bill Coulter (Staff Sergeant William M.) always thanks me for the hatch cover. He said he laid on top of it and hung onto a raft until his rescue. Just think how many stories could be told about those years in the Army. I spent four and one-half years from beginning to the end.

"Last of all, most important, I want to thank the crew of the USS McCalla. All of us were new to the horrors of war, but each man carried out his duty. There was a comradeship the existed through all the armed forces in those days. We know we could rely on each other when help was needed. It was a special feeling I will never forget.

"I remember landing on Fiji and an honor guard stood at attention as we came off the ship. All of the allied forces banded together to whip the Axis, and they did."

1st Fighter Control Squadron Casualties from the Sinking of SS Cape San Juan Coming Ashore

Cape San Juan survivors coming ashore from YMS-241 on November 14th, 1943. Survivor in center is as yet unidentified. Officer to left staring directly at the camera is identified as Colonel George Finney, Commanding officer of the 18th General Hospital, supervising the work of bringing the survivors ashore. Photo by T/5 Salvadore Tesoriero. Photo courtesy of the Rutherford B. Hayes Presidential Center; Colonel Stanley Wolfe Collection. Note that it was raining at the time.

There are no records of any 1st Fighter Control Squadron members being interviewed by the Coast Guard or Navy investigators. However in Captain Miller's hastily written "history notes" he says of the Martin Mariner rescue, "(They) rescued some twenty members of this organization's personnel. These men were flown to Suva, Fiji."

Some of the men were rescued by Edwin T. Meredith and were dropped off at Noumea, New Caledonia, and the balance of the rescued 1st Fighters were picked up the following morning after the Mariner mission by the USS McCalla and also taken to Suva.

That day the 1st Fighter Control Squadron lost "in action" one officer and nine enlisted men:

Killed:
>Sergeant James O. Clowdus
>Private First Class Charles E. Miner

Missing (presumed KIA):
>2nd Lieutenant Stanley O. McDonald
>Sergeant Edmund A. Cannon
>Corporal Wilbur A. Barger
>Corporal William L. Darsey
>Corporal Richard P. Hergenrather
>Corporal Max F. Wilkans
>Private First Class Benjamin E. Keen
>Private First Class Rosario A. Mocciaro

Wounded:
The entire organization (suffered exposure and fuel oil to the eyes as well as the broken bones and lacerations of some.)

At Suva most of the men were hospitalized and treated for exhaustion, exposure and for oil-filled eyes. The effect of oil in the eyes proved to be the worse casualty agent.

Captain Miller's notes also reflect,
>"The high caliber of the men in the organization is definitely proven by the manner in which all operations during the horrible night in the water was executed. Each

raft was loaded to three or four times its capacity. In most every case a raft was found to be in command of men of this organization."

Technical Sergeant James L. Cox of the 1st Fighter Control Squadron was cited by the Navy and the Commanding General of the Fifth Air force for,

To wit:
>"The excellency of his leadership of the raft on which he and sixty men spent twenty-six hours."

Many other men demonstrated heroic actions that day which have never been made a part of public record.

Survivors Taken To Noumea, Suva
—and on to Brisbane, Australia

The men on Noumea arrived 16 November 1943 and were taken to the 6th Replacement Depot. The Men who landed on Suva departed there on 26 November 1943, arriving on Noumea on the 28th. All but the ten men left in hospital in Suva, embarked on 2 December 1942 aboard the SS Willard A. Hollbrook, arriving in Brisbane, Australia, on 7 December.

There they were staged at the 5th Replacement Depot where they obtained new supplies and equipment, new records made, and general preparations done for further movement to the war.

On Christmas Eve the members were provided with Christmas carols played over the loudspeakers, group singing and games and a canned turkey dinner for Christmas Day 1943.

Corporal Augusta L. Bray recalls post-sinking experiences,

"A few days later we left Fiji aboard a hospital ship bound for New Caledonia where we were issued some clothes and a partial payment in two-dollar bills. After two or three days we moved on to Brisbane, Australia, to regroup.

"My Granddad gave me a Parker fountain pen in 1938 for pulling weeds out of his alfalfa, and I carried it through four years of high school. The day before the Cape San Juan was torpedoed, I loaned it to one of the

60

guys to write home. In the chow line one night at Ascot, Australia he returned it to me. I thought it was (Staff Sergeant Clarence E.) Luetkemeyer, but he denies it. If anyone of you guys remembers this story I'd like to know—I still have the old Parker!"

Technical Sergeant Chester Driest,
"On 13 January 1944, the second anniversary of the activation of the 1st Fighter Control Squadron, a squadron party was held at the mess hall of the 11th Replacement Battalion, Camp Ascot. A special dinner with beer was served and a program for the occasion was held after the meal. The month of January was spent staging, training, and preparing for further movement."

Corporal Augusta L. Bray, added a thought,
"On 23 February 1944 the 1st Fighter Control Squadron, having survived a ship sinking and many debilitating injuries, and the rigors of reorganization and rearming finally, got alerted for 'water movement to the north.'"

Anonymous,
"I remember that the officers bought a bunch of booze, had it crated and labelled *Medical Stores*, and loaded it onto the Cape San Juan—where it all ended up on the bottom of the ocean. Those officers tried again at Brisbane, bought booze, and crated it as *Medical Stores*. But when we got to

Finschhafen it had all been stolen by a bunch of merchant mariners.

"The enlisted men had sense enough to store their acquisitions in their barracks bags—where they could keep an eye on it."

Corporal William Klein,

"In January 1945, while we were still in Brisbane, Australia, about twenty of us were sent to Finschhafen, New Guinea—the first group to leave Brisbane for special assignments in the theater of war. We flew to Rockhampton, Australia, stayed overnight, and the next morning took off for Finschhafen.

"On the way, both wings caught fire, but the pilot managed to get us over the ocean to Finschhafen. When we hit the runway, both wingtips drooped to within a foot of the runway. After the plane was unloaded, a bulldozer nudged it into the junk yard.

"Besides me, the other guys (on the flight) were George Ashcraft, Leo Goldberg, Frank Jaco, and a cryptographer who was transferred to the 1st Fighter at March Field following duty in Panama. We installed an FM radio station on Cape Gloucester to serve Finschhafen, which took us until the end of May, by which time the entire squadron was at Finschhafen, staging for Hollandia and Wakde."

First War Assignment—Finschhafen

Sailing 6 March 1944, the unit arrived at Finschhafen, Papua New Guinea, on 16 March.

Corporal Augusta L. Bray notes,
"We reorganized with new clothes, personal gear, and new hand tools. I left Brisbane with the squadron headed for Finschhafen, New Guinea. I remember that a lot of us got raincoats marked:
Not For Use In Tropics.

"Our hand tools were Australian—and metric—pretty useless on American vehicles. Seems everything had to be modified somehow. Torn off brake lines were a problem. We had no parts and no brake fluid. We'd plug a hole in a line and use mosquito repellent for brake fluid. Shear pins in wrenches broke so we used screwdriver shafts. We hacked of governors on trucks to get them through mud holes. Aircraft and vehicle dumps became major parts sources for us.

"Before we could get comfortable with jungle life, word came to install waterproof kits on five trucks and two Jeeps in preparation for assault landing on Hollandia, New Guinea."

Staff Sergeant William M. "Bill" Coulter,

"While we were waiting in Finschhafen, New Guinea, for the actions to come, the squadron was assigned the task of establishing communications between Finschhafen and Aitape, New Guinea, by FM radio.

"This entailed establishing a radio outpost on Umboi Island, one-hundred ten miles from Finschhafen off the western end of New Britain. The only briefing we got about Umboi was some air recon photos and a map.

"Umboi Island is about thirty miles long, ten miles wide, swampy and mountainous, with a couple of abandoned plantations. We were also told it had been occupied by Japs, but the intelligence people thought they had left. They thought! Our communications officer Captain Johnson, said, 'If you run into trouble, come back.' He didn't explain exactly how we were to do this.

"The trip took two days by landing craft. We located the beach where we were to set up and by nightfall we were in business, and in communication with Finschhafen. The next morning the little flotilla headed back to Finschhafen, leaving five of us on Umboi—myself, Sergeant Leo Goldberg, Virgil Green, Harvey Scott, and another guy who was a lineman or pole climber. I cannot recall his name, but he was a tall redhead who amused the natives with his antics in trying to take a shower in a helmet full of water.

"It soon developed that it was a sanitary necessity to have a latrine rather than use a shovel every time nature called. I undertook to explain to a couple of natives the nature of our requirement. I had learned some Pigeon English from an Australian who was on the island as the representative of his government, and I thought I got pretty good at it.

"Frank, the Australian, was not around, so I had to handle the natives by myself. He had assigned the two natives to us to 'kelp out,' clear the grounds, get water, etc.— *Broom-broom dis place*. They had been given some training by a missionary and had some primitive tools to work with.

"The Pigeon English name for toilet is *House Peek Peek*. But I had forgotten the term, and was trying to explain to *ERO*—he had his name tattooed on his chest—that we wanted him and his friend, *AGUS*, to move an outhouse from where it sat some distance away to a point closer to us. Frank had told me that it could be moved.

ERO stood there with a puzzled look on his face trying to figure out what I was saying. I tried various terms: big house with a little house out back—outhouse—two holer— chick sales—I just couldn't remember *House Peek Peek*. For thirty minutes I was not even close to getting through to *ERO*. Finally Virgil Green emerged from the tent and said, 'Let me try.' He unbuckled his belt, lowered his pants, and squatted. *ERO*'s response was instant, 'Sure Shit House.' Virgil and I collapsed on the ground laughing. *ERO* must have thought we were *long-long*, pigeon for crazy.

"Frank told me later that they never used *House Peek Peek* to describe a latrine—not on Umboi. But I learned something that day. If you want to communicate and be understood: *KEEP IT SIMPLE.*

"After 45 days we returned to Finschhafen. Leo and Virgil got so sick that the unit had to come and get them a couple of weeks earlier. We were replaced there by a group of about thirty Signal Corps people. The natives came to see us off, saying *Sorry to Miss,* and giving me a salute that said I was *Number One Master.* They stood on the rocks waving until we were out of sight.

Oh, Memories."

There was no assigned mission at Finschhafen, but on 12 April 1944 while the squadron was staging, Captain McBride, commanding officer at that time, received a secret field order to: "Form four detachments, A, B, C, and rear echelon, in preparation for the D-Day landing operation at Hollandia."

Chapter Four

BATTLE OF HOLLANDIA

Code Name Operation *Reckless*
(New Guinea Campaign, spring of 1944)

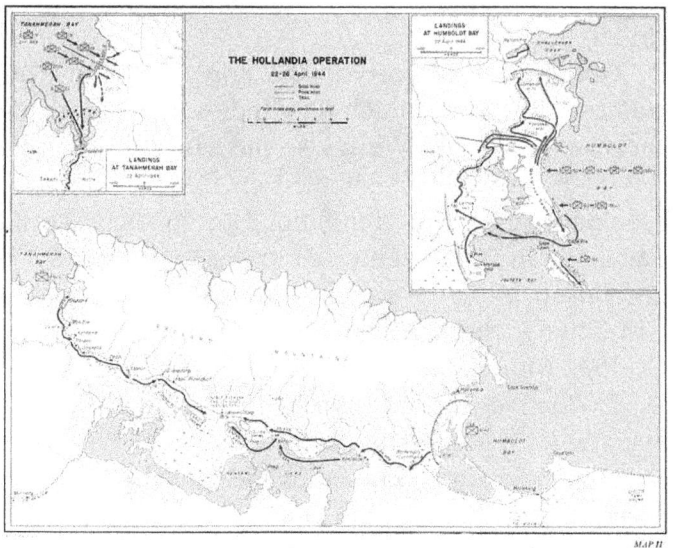

General Douglas MacArthur used Allied air and naval superiority to land troops where the Japanese were weakest, seeking to confine the stronger

Japanese forces to pockets from which they could not break out due to natural terrain obstacles and the Allied control of air and sea. The next nine months of 1944 were devoted to this strategy.

Capture of the Admiralties at the end of February 1944 isolated Rabaul on the island of New Britain, the largest island in the Bismarck Archipelago of Papua New Guinea, and gave MacArthur a forward air base that extended his fighter range past Wewak, the capital of East Sepik province and the site of the largest Japanese airbase in mainland New Guinea. He took advantage of the superior position and battle resources by ordering a change in plans that would leapfrog 400 miles up the New Guinea coastline to capture the major Japanese air and supply base at Hollandia.

Hollandia is a port on the north coast of New Guinea, part of the Dutch East Indies, and is the only anchorage between Wewak to the east and Geelvink Bay to the west. It is situated on the east side of a headland separating Humboldt Bay to the east and Tanahmerah Bay, twenty-five miles to the west. The town itself is on the shore of Humboldt Bay, with a first-class anchorage. The headland is formed by the Cyclops Mountains, a mountain ridge rising steeply to 7,000 feet and is backed by Lake Sentani, extending fifteen miles east to west.

Hollandia was occupied by the invading Japanese during the invasion of the Dutch East Indies in 1942 and became a base for their expansion to the east towards the Australian mandated territories of Papua New Guinea. Between the above described mountain ridge and the lake was a narrow plain, where the Japanese had built a number of airfields. Three had been completed by April 1944 and a fourth was under construction.

In the spring of 1944 the Allied South West Pacific Command determined that the area should be seized and developed into a staging post for their advance along the north coast of New Guinea into the Dutch East Indies and to the Philippines.

Sixty B-24 heavy bombers, escorted by long-range P-38s, went against Hollandia on 30 March, demolishing nearly all the Japanese aircraft and ending any threat to the Allies from the sky over New Guinea. A well-designed deception effort kept the Japanese expecting a blow at the Madang-Hansa area while the true focus shifted to the west at Hollandia and Aitape, splitting the Japanese forces on New Guinea in half.

18 April 1944—En Route to Hollandia

At 0530, five officers and fifty-one enlisted men of the *1ˢᵗ Fighter Control Squadron Detachment A* loaded up and headed for Hollandia. Under the command of **Lieutenant Edward M. Bonfoey**, it was scheduled to participate in *Operation Letterpress*, the designation of the Humboldt Bay part of the overall Hollandia *Operation Reckless*. Bonfoey's mission is to establish early air raid warning and control anti-aircraft fire and Navy and Air Corps fighter planes at Humboldt Bay, designated *Shadow*, during the operation.

21 April 1944—New Guinea

A United States task force commanded by Vice Admiral Mitscher and including aircraft carriers, battleships, cruisers, and destroyers brings aerial and naval bombardment to bear on Japanese airfields and defense installations in the area of Hollandia, Wakde Island, Sawar, and Sarmi. No significant air opposition was encountered while many enemy aircraft were destroyed on the ground. The attack, continuing through the night, was in preparation for the landing on the 22nd.

22 April 1944—New Guinea

First light in the Hollandia area disclosed a heavily overcast sky from which a light drizzle intermittently fell upon the ships bearing the *Reckless Task Force* toward its objectives. The weather gave no promise that aircraft aboard the carriers of Task Force 58, standing offshore between Humboldt and Tanahmerah Bays, would be able to execute all their assigned support missions. On the other hand, the weather conditions aided Allied forces, for the approach of the convoys to Hollandia was at least partially concealed from Japanese eyes. Chances for local surprise seemed excellent.

The 7th Amphibious Force commanded by Rear Admiral Barbey and carrying 81,000 men supported by the aircraft and naval guns of Task Force 58, prepared to go ashore.

The opposing force of Japanese, commanded by the 18th Imperial Japanese Army's General Hatazo Adachi, numbered 11,000 men.

The Allied landings by the U.S. Sixth Army began at 0700 with one regiment going ashore at

Aitape, east of Hollandia, and two divisions landing in Humboldt Bay and Tanahmerah Bay.

The 1st Fighter Control Squadron Detachment A, under the command of **Lieutenant Edward M. Bonfoey**, went ashore with the first wave of infantry in the Humboldt Bay segment of the overall Hollandia *Operation Reckless*, and Bonfoey quickly established the facility for early enemy air raid warning, control of anti-aircraft fire, and Navy and Air Corps fighter planes at Humboldt Bay.

This was the mission of the 1st Fighter Control Squadron, built on long training, innovation, and survival at sea.

Bonfoey's Detachment A was designated *Shadow* during the operation. In addition to 1st Fighter Control Squadron personnel, a Navy controller was assigned to the detachment to control Navy aircraft during the operation through the use of Detachment A facilities. During initial approach to the beach the Navy controller used their communications equipment mounted on a 6x6 truck on the deck of LST 118 to direct Navy aircraft, providing necessary air cover during the assault landing.

Corporal Augusta L. Bray, now a truck driver with Bonfoey's Detachment A, reported,

> "The naval bombardment for the pre-dawn landing was second to few fireworks shows. Tensions relaxed as men and equipment reached the beach. Once on the beach our first problem was, 'Where do we go?' We had landed on top of a Japanese supply dump with row after row of 600-pound bombs, barrels of fuel,

aircraft engines, guns, ammunition—even food supplies—with no road going out and completely surrounded by a swamp six-ten feet deep and over a hundred yards across. Engineers piled trees, barrels and anything they could find to make a crossing over the swamp. We tied trucks to bulldozers and dragged them to dry ground.

"Once across the swamp we moved up the side of Pancake Hill and started setting up equipment. I went back to the beach for more equipment—and saw my first Jap casualties. I watched as a small group of sailors tried to take a little rocky knoll a few yards out in the bay. It looked like they couldn't find a way to get out of their barge as they began to take enemy fire. An infantry patrol went out and after a few well-placed grenades the sailors leaped out of the barge and stormed the rocks. Minutes later Jap bodies began to be thrown over the rocks into the bay. I headed back up the hill.

"Soon after dark we heard Japanese planes were on radar headed our way. With no specific duty I went into my foxhole to await their arrival. Soon we heard the planes and instantly saw machine-gun tracer fire. I dropped deep into my hole—and all hell broke loose. One blast followed another. Hunkered down, heart pounding, waiting and wondering how long this will last, I heard voices. Raising up I saw the Jap supply dump on fire just seventy-five yards away. This was our first bombing—with many more to come. The next night Jap Zekes dropped 'daisy-cutters' and incendiaries into our camp. Luckily we got only one injury."

Sergeant Norman N "Pop" Satin,

"I was one of the men chosen by Captain Bonfoey to go with him in the advance detail that hit the beach in the Hollandia operation. We went in with the first wave of infantry and got our ground-to-air radio control system up and working.

"Shortly after landing on Hollandia, General MacArthur and his staff, cameras grinding and the front of his LST dropping just before hitting shore, strode into the surf and up on the beach. MacArthur got his pants wet up to the knees. He had all the GIs in sight line up in single file so that he could pass in review, stop to shake hands with guys, and congratulate us for a job well done."

"General Kruger came along behind MacArthur's group and gave us orders to pick up supplies and lumber along the beach to clean up the area. A few of us complied, but as soon as the general was out of sight we dropped the lumber and junk and took off."

Rough going at Tanahmerah Bay

Assault ships of the Western Attack Group, carrying the 24th Infantry Division to Tanahmerah Bay, anchored some 10,000 yards off *RED Beach 2*, about a mile farther than planned. This change was due to bad weather which obscured landmarks expected by ships' pilots to guide them to the proper anchorages.

Landing craft approaching Tanahmerah Bay

Troops of the 24th Division quickly breakfasted and assault personnel then began clambering down nets into waiting landing craft of the 542d Engineer Boat and Shore Regiment. The transfer to small craft, although hampered by rough seas in the transport area, was completed about 0535 and the leading waves formed rapidly.

The mission of Bonfoey's Detachment A was completed when the 31st fighter subsector (*CAMPHOR*) landed at Tanahmerah Bay, twenty miles west of *Shadow*, and became operational with control over the air strip and ready to signal air raid warnings, direct fighter aircraft and anti-aircraft fire.

23 April 1944—New Guinea

The Americans occupied Hollandia without opposition, advancing along a line from Pim to Lake Dentani. The beaches at Tanahmerah became congested, forcing a follow up convoy that was due the next day to be redirected to Humboldt Bay instead.

One regiment reached the village of Sabron, passing through it until they reached a nearby stream. Here they met the first organized resistance by the Japanese and the Americans withdrew to the village.

The troops that landed in the Aitape area occupied Tadji airfield and pushed toward Hollandia to join up with the main body of the US invasion force.

25 April 1944—New Guinea

Reinforcements and supplies land in Humboldt Bay. In the Aitape area, the US 186th Infantry

Regiment advanced as far as Nefaar, beyond Lake Sentani. American patrols carried out thrusts to the east towards Wewak and to the west towards Hollandia (*now known as Jayapurna*).

26 April 1944—New Guinea

American engineers reopened airfields at Hollandia and Aitape. The pincers closed on Hollandia and the few surviving Japanese fled to the jungle in hopes of reaching Sarmi, about 150 miles to the northwest.

28 April 1944—Letters Home

Lieutenant Edward Monroe Bonfoey—three personal letters home. The first, written 28 April to his parents, recorded his first combat landing experience (Hollandia assault):

> "As you probably have guessed due to not hearing from me, I have been on a big assault landing here. Had a lot of fun and am now out of danger. I have been wearing Jap uniforms, eating Jap rice, canned fish, tea, cocoa and using Jap soap. Have drunk some captured Jap apple cider. We really took the booty. Have seen some dead Japs and plenty of captured ones. They had some missionaries—American and Dutch—and were they glad to see the Americans!

"I can't mention anything accept in general but we really took the Japs down a peg. MacArthur and Halsey were here three hours after we landed and I saw both of them. I don't want you to worry, for any Japs left on New Guinea haven't much fight in them. I got my wish and have been in the front lines with the infantry so to speak, so now will be taking it easy for a while.

"I am enclosing a little Nip money. I have all the booty in the world but will probably leave it here. I even have been eating Jap candy and sugar and salt tablets (all this is naturally checked by our doctors for purity). My mail may be very slow and also I haven't had time to write for a couple of weeks and probably won't have time to write only about once a week from now on for the next month. I am well, but as I am commanding officer of this unit it really keeps me busy and although I will be safe, I won't have much time. The climate here is pleasant and everyone busy. Saw my first white women in a long while, Dutch missionaries."

Bonfoey's next letter, dated 1 May, 1944, had enclosed some Japanese money printed in English in anticipation of the time when the Japanese would take Australia. Bonfoey noted that they also used it to pay the natives in New Guinea.

"More and more prisoners are coming in. I can't say how many. Also plenty of Indian Sikh troops captured at Singapore and brought here and used for forced labor. Also more white missionaries. They really are happy to be saved. These Nips are no hari-kari boys now. They don't seem to mind being captured which is a good sign. I have a Jap bicycle and plenty of Jap uniforms, also a parachute, guns and other odds and ends but guess I will leave them here.

"You probably have read a lot in the papers about the blow here as we have heard the Frisco news over the radio. I was up the first 70 hours here straight and haven't had a bath other than in the ocean since I've been here, but I am now able to get some sleep. I have named my jeep "Flying Jackass" and it really pushed through the mud."

Lieutenant Bonfoey wrote a third letter on 6 May, posted 11 May, which "came through in excellent time," his parents noted.

"Not much news. Hope to get back to my mail before long. Am well and busy. Sure will be glad to get some clean clothes and to a shower (open air or barrel) and hope I will before long. We are in a healthy spot on a hill overlooking the ocean. We have no tents, etc., to speak of. However everyone is getting along okay.

"In my unit only had one boy wounded so we were lucky. Surely hope things pop in Europe … Doesn't look like they need much more over there to keep moving fast. Sure hope we can keep making big jumps from now on."

April 1944—New Guinea

Technical Sergeant Mitchell Williamson,
"On 12 April 1944 we were ordered to form detachments whose personnel would take part in advance area D-Day landings with assault forces. Detachment A was to establish early warning and control AAA fire and Navy and Army fighters at Humboldt Bay during the *Letterpress* operation (Hollandia, Indonesia area). Men were well briefed en route, so all went well during the landing except for a brief communications break when our antenna was wrenched from a truck as a bulldozer towed it through a native hut on the beach (necessary due to a serious traffic jam on the beach road).

"At Tanahmerah Bay the 31st Fighter Subsector *Camphor* was delayed in setting up by another traffic jam of men, equipment, and vehicles on a swamp-flanked beach, so our (1st Fighters) *Shadow* installation served both as a fighter control sector and relay station until Camphor was finally operational in Pim Hill on 30 April.

"Four *red alerts* were called in the first nine days at Shadow, three on actual bogies, one on a B-24 doing night recon. On 23 April a single-seater enemy fighter hit an ammo dump near Shadow with four light bombs, and explosions continued intermittently for five days. A second raid on Pancake Hill, with no advance warning, killed seven men and wounded forty-two—one being a member of the *Shadow* crew."

The mission of the 1st Fighter Control Squadron Detachments A and B were accomplished on Hollandia.

Their next action was the D-Day landing on Wakde Island on 17 May 1944.

Chapter Five

Battle of Wakde
(Operation Straight Line)

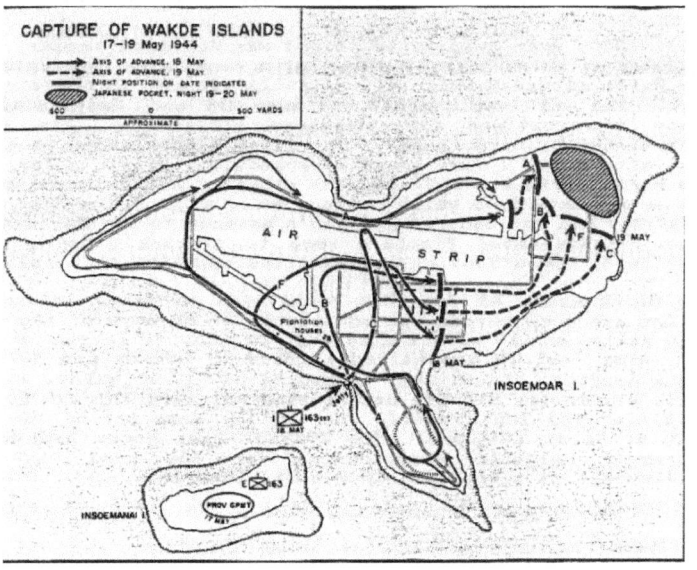

Differences in the execution of the Pacific operations between General Douglas MacArthur and Admiral Chester Nimitz had President Roosevelt dividing the commands. Nimitz struck the Japanese up the central Pacific using naval units and aircraft carriers, and MacArthur leapfrogged along the New

Guinea coast, across the Moluccas New Celebes Islands, and on to the Philippines.

Because of this divided command, MacArthur lost the support of the carriers for most of his remaining operations. Hollandia had been intended to become a heavy bomber base, but presented two difficult conditions. It was now further from intended targets, and it didn't have soil that could support the weight of heavy bombers.

Wakde, on the other hand, had a shorter runway, but a coral base so it became the central bomber base. Aircraft from commands further down the New Guinea coast could now fly to Wakde, refuel, load bombs, and hit targets along the route of attack.

The 1st Fighter Control Squadron gained additional duties as a Bomber/Fighter Control Squadron. They now had the tasks of Early Warning, Anti-Aircraft Fire Control, and Long Range Bomber Control. Additionally, the 1st Fighters controlled medium bomber/fighter low-level bombing and strafing missions in the Sarni Point area, attack missions at Biak, Sansapore, Morotia, and the Celebes Sea area. They controlled long range bomb attacks at Yap, Ngulu, and Palau Islands.

Some missions were beyond the design limits of the B-24 bombers, and Air Force personnel made modifications in the field to keep them on track. The 1st Fighter Control Squadron addressed the challenge of the long distance communications requirements by modifying HF (High Frequency) transmitters to provide 1000 watts of power, facilitation voice communications for the entire mission. They also provided communications with PBY Catalinas and submarines to pick up crew members who had ditched crippled aircraft, and provided homing for aircraft returning from missions with trouble with flight instruments. The squadron saved many lives, as well as valuable aircraft. Another innovation they created was a method to synchronize ac power generators to allow transfer of electrical power without interruption of communications.

6 May 1944—Wakde Island, New Guinea

Rear Admiral Barby had advised that the start of operations to land on Sarmi and Wakde Island be put back from its scheduled 15 May to 21 May 1944. General Douglas MacArthur counters, and the landings on Wakde Island from which air forces will be able to protect the future landing on Biak Island stays as planned.

16 May 1944

Task Force Tornado sailed from Hollandia for the occupation of Wakde Island. The consolidation of the Hollandia beachheads continues. But this leap forward has cost the Allies 1,060 dead and 4,000 wounded. The Japanese have suffered 9,000 dead and at least 650 taken prisoner.

17 May 1944

The Wakde-Sarmi region, beginning about 140 miles west of Hollandia, had been developed by the Japanese into a ground and air position of considerable strategic importance. There were good airfields at Mafin and Sawar on the mainland and on Wakde Island itself just off the New Guinea shore opposite Toem. The Japanese had established numerous bivouac and storage areas along the entire coastal road from Maffin Bay to Sarmi. Intelligence sources indicated that the enemy was concentrated in strength in the Wakde-Sarmi region. It was therefore decided to employ a division less one regimental combat team at Sarmi and use the regimental team for the seizure of Wakde Island.

After the successful landing operation on Hollandia, the next leapfrog landed unopposed in Maffin Bay near Sarmi Village on 17 May 1944 and took the small Wakde Island after three days of unexpectedly heavy fighting.

Following a technique already used on many occasions, guns had been landed with a regiment of infantry near Arare on the coast of Dutch New Guinea across from the main landings, and proceed to lay down systematic fire on the main objectives at Wakde. Stubborn resistance from a strongly entrenched enemy was encountered but by 20 May all opposition had been overcome and the airdrome cleared for use.

Other units occupied the islet of Inumania not manned by Japanese forces.

An attempt on Sarmi Village, about eighteen miles west of the beachhead, was held up by an effective Japanese defense and threatened counterattack. Lone Tree Hill, the high ground dominating Maffin Bay, was finally taken by reinforcements on 24 June, but scattered resistance continued through the end of 1944.

The fighting near Sarmi cost U.S. Army units approximately 2,100 battle casualties, while over 10,000 Japanese perished.

Task Force 77, commanded by Rear Admiral William Fechteler, supported by USS Stockton covered the Wakde landing on 17 May 1944 by the 2nd Engineer Special Brigade, Company A, 542nd Engineer Boat and Shore Regiment of the 163rd Regimental Combat Team of the 41st Infantry Division. After a three-day battle the island was declared captured on 18 May. The capture of Wakde cost the Americans 40 killed and 107 wounded. The Japanese lost 759 killed and 4 captured.

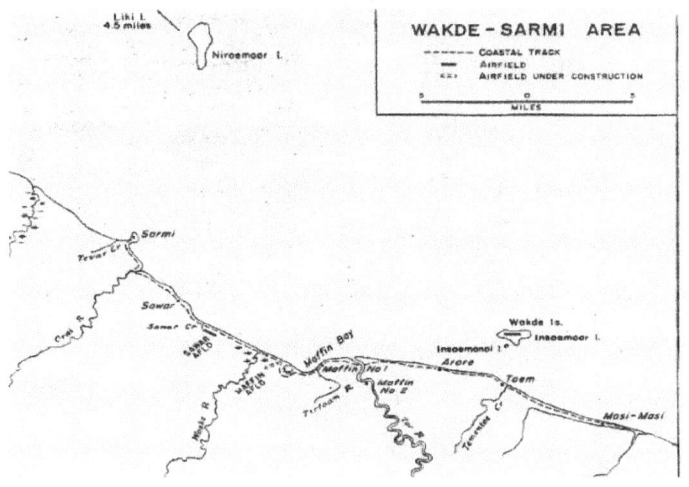

The 1ˢᵗ Fighter Control Squadron detached personnel who participated in April's *Shadow* operation on Hollandia, now landed at Kebon Village on Wakde Island on 17 May, 1944, and were designated *Goblet* Fighter Control Center.

The Kebon landing was beset by unloading difficulties, but by 1735 that day communications operations were up and running in a squad tent. Troop movement information during the first several days was poor. During the night of the 18ᵗʰ a Field Artillery unit released a balloon. Triple A (anti-aircraft guns) fired upon it and triggered a false *red alert*. Reports received by *Shadow* from the Triple A positions were unreliable as witnessed by one in which an "approaching enemy barge" turned out to be a floating log. In another case reports of aircraft motors heard were traced to friendly surface craft.

Goblet relayed messages from the Air Liaison Party, *Manner*, to aircraft, directing bombing and strafing missions, all completed without mishap.

"Main Street" on Wakde Island

23 May 1944—New Guinea

On 23 May *Goblet* completed its mission and operations were transferred to *1ˢᵗ Fighter Control Squadron Detachment B* at the Wrecker Fighter Control Center on *Insoemanai Island*—called "little Wakde." The island is about 3,500 yards off *Wakde's* southern shore.

Detachment B, commanded by Lieutenant Alfred R. Kennickell, consisted of four officers and sixteen enlisted men, had departed from Finschhafen on 12 May 1944 by air. They flew to a staging point in the Aitape area where they billeted with the 303ʳᵈ Airdrome Squadron. As it developed, the higher echelons on Aitape had no knowledge of Detachment B, 1ˢᵗ Fighter Control Squadron, and after consultation with Task Force Headquarters, the 1ˢᵗ Fighters were embarked 13 May on an LST (Landing Ship Tank) with all of their equipment. The LST sailed from Aitape in convoy the evening of 14 May, arriving at Hollandia the next day. Later that day the detachment's commanding officer contacted Detachment A.

Rendezvousing at Tanahmerah Bay on Hollandia, Detachment B proceeded toward Wakde. Shortly after H-Hour of D-Day, 17 May, they landed in the Kebon Village area and spent the night with Bonfoey's Detachment A.

Fighting still raged on Wakde Island, and on the 19ᵗʰ they moved to *Insoemanai*.

The 32ⁿᵈ Fighter Control Subsector was erected by 22 May and Detachment B took over *Goblet's* operations, reinforced by some of Detachment A's people. In all of these moves, the fragile radio equipment of the 1st Fighters was loaded and unloaded five times.

On 31 May the rest of the 1st Fighter Control Squadron began loading at Finschhafen aboard SS John Burroughs bound for *Insoemanai.*

Recollections of 1st Fighters of Hollandia Operations

(The rest of the 1ˢᵗ Fighters sailed from Finschhafen aboard SS John Burroughs on 1 June 1944, arriving at Wakde Island 6 June.)

"We sailed on the *Burroughs* 1 June 1944, all accommodations extremely crowded and equipment jamming the deck space. Many men slept topside and mess duty was shared with the units aboard. The convoy trip was uneventful.

"On sailing day the subsector received a radiogram from V Fighter Command General Paul Wurtsmith congratulating our detachment for their excellent work establishing aircraft warning and control in the Wakde Island area. On 6 June the ship anchored near Wakde and the men were barged to *Insoemanai.* Temporary camp was set up, work starting about 2230. At 2400 enemy aircraft dropped a few bombs.

"Permanent camp construction began the next day, which also marked the arrival of Captain Donald A. Dake, our new commanding officer for the 1st Fighter Control Squadron. In spite of supply problems the 32nd Fighter Sector was complete and fully operational by 26 June—five days before the deadline. We experienced five air raids during June without casualties.

"As a Fighter/Bomber Control Squadron we were very active in the Wakde operations, with missions at Kabon-Sarmi area, Yap, Palau, the Celebes, and the Philippine Island area. Our squadron performed with professionalism. The 'on-the-job' training of Captain Bolick, Captain 'Do As It Is, By God' Miller and others paid off with a fraternal devotion to the squadron and to each officer and enlisted man. (*After surviving the sinking*) We were the Fighting First again.

"Remember when some of us ran out of uniforms at Hollandia and we grabbed some Japanese uniforms from one of the supply dumps. It was a little unnerving for the guys in the control tent at Wakde to see a rump in a Jap uniform backing into the center—but like so many other things, we just got used to it.

"One event that we all recall is the night on Wakde when one guy got stoned on some alcoholic concoction then circulating around—and I really mean stoned. But he was smiling gently and some of the fellows laid him quietly in an empty radio case, put some palm branches over him, folded his hands across his chest, and lit a candle at the foot of the radio case. And that is the way he woke up in the morning, along with a brutal headache. Several guys since have claimed to be the person who earned immortality that night, including *you know who*. But we know the real identity of this person—and he shall remain forever unnamed, but a legend in his own time."

The Flying Circus

At Wakde Island a number of squadron members were abruptly transferred to a new unit, the 5297th Airborne Fighter Control Squadron, tagged *The Flying Circus*. An obvious forerunner of the AWACS (Airborne Warning and Control System) mission of the modern Air Force. The *Flying Circus* operated equipment and a control center from a C-47 aircraft. If you know the C-47, the guys must have worked in very close quarters.

Typical Douglas C-47 Skytrain

Donald A. Dake

The New Commanding Office

Succeeding McBride on 16 June 1944, then Captain and ultimately Major **Donald A. Dake** led the *1ˢᵗ Fighter Control Squadron* for the rest of the war.

There are no official descriptions of his work, nor any personal writings from Dake on record. However, Chester Driest managed to acquire a most revealing essay from one of his squadron mates.

Sergeant Stephen H. Loeb writes,

"A crowd of several hundred soldiers sat, crouched, or stood in the open space on Wakde Island off the New Guinea coast. We were assembled in an area hacked out of a grove of coconut trees. Each corner of the opening was anchored by a ramshackle structure consisting of the screened-in mess hall, the chapel, the headquarters building, and the large control center with its plotting section.

"A hush fell over this motley crew as a tall, handsome, and imposing officer stepped forward. His ruddy complexion was tinted by the yellow stain of atropine, a sign that he'd been in the jungle longer than any of us. Although his shirt bore the insignia of captain, it had started to come apart at the shoulder seams. Immediately he flashed a warm, engaging smile as he commenced, for the first time, to address his new command."

Captain Dake said,

"I was ready to go home, when I was offered the challenge of taking over this command. You are all aware of what I am confronting and what happened in the past, but with your help and cooperation we will transform this highly technical unit into a dedicated group that has a sense of purpose for their mission in this theater of war. I don't have the training, nor the skills that most of you possess, nor do I profess to be familiar with the functions of a Fighter Control Squadron. Yet I will endeavor to motivate you, to change your attitude so that you will carry out the task for which you were trained and brought here to perform. Always remember, we are in this war together."

Sergeant Stephen H. Loeb reflected,

"I could feel the tension and anticipation that hovered over the assembly evaporate with his every word."

Captain Dake continued,

"All I expect of you is that you give your best during your assigned duty hours and carry out your job to the best of your ability. Yet, when you are idle, I encourage you to make the most of your existence in this forsaken part of the world. By all means, use your imagination to improve your lot, your living quarters, your well-being, while you are a soldier over here. Therefore, all unnecessary ceremonial military functions will be dispensed with."

Sergeant Loeb continues his report,

"Spontaneous cheers and applause broke out. Our quest for a change had been answered. We were starved for real leadership, where discipline would be elicited through respect and admiration, rather than fear and punishment. After this gathering was dismissed, he invited us all to a weenie roast in the mess hall. The rare ingredients for the feast had accompanied him on the airplane.

"That, in essence, is how I remember the historic evening and the first handshake with Donald Dake. But I will never forget how I was the only witness to his arrival in camp that morning, and how I broadcast the news to everyone within earshot as I ran through the rows of tents we had pitched on Insoemanai Island. From then on, in the squadron orderly room I had a front row seat in observing our commanding officer in action every day.

"But that day, and the tenor of his speech which changed our lives, will always stand out in my recollections of his successful command. How can we forget the granting of an often-denied furlough from New Guinea to far-away Melbourne, Australia? Or my full-body blush when standing in the nude and saluting a covey of the highest ranking Air Corps generals as they stopped by my boat—a craft I had fashioned from a discarded wing tank. Word got around about how well we were operating and our unit was rewarded with many citations, ranking first in the Pacific theater among Fighter Control Squadrons."

(Ed note: Dake's promotion to Major followed swiftly.)

"Although Major Dake was not with us on the Cape San Juan, he truly became one of us during the relentless three-day kamikaze attack on our convoy while we were traveling from Leyte to Mindoro in the Philippines. Our loaded LST seemed particularly vulnerable. This engagement, often treated secondarily during our reminiscing at reunions, came within seconds and a few yards of wiping out the greatest part of our squadron. From my vantage point, spread out in a hammock strung from the floor of one of our turrets, I gave a running account of the action to everyone huddled below and under the vehicles on the deck. The ship directly behind us was sunk with all hands. Major Dake was visibly relieved that we were spared this fate. His concern was getting us home safely, and he never used us as pawns for personal glory. His leadership had forged us into a team of dedicated individuals and soldiers."

Stephen H. Loeb concluded his remarks with,

"The day that Donald Dake became our commanding officer was the turning point in the lives of a collection of shattered spirits, who, at the outset of their journey to the Pacific Theater of War had suffered the agonies and tribulations of human beings, exposed to hours of terror, cold and loneliness, drifting abandoned in the ocean in a fight for basic survival. Two years later, he returned us to the United States as proud veterans who had accomplished their mission with distinction. For that we are forever grateful, and salute our commanding officer, Major Donald A. Dake."

(Ed. note: The feelings expressed above by Loeb about Donald Dake are also found in many other remarks.

The only mention of the negative attitude the troops seem to have had of the previous CO, and what happened to him, are found in notes by Technical Sergeant Arthur K. Berkey:

"... Both assault landings (Hombolt Bay and Kebon Village—Wakde) were under the command of Captain Bonfoey. Captain McBride had been placed on temporary assignment following a request to the Inspector General's Office by the entire squadron, alleging his inability to command a combat unit. On 6 June, McBride was relieved

of command by Captain Don Dake. On orders of President Roosevelt, Captain Dake served as our commanding officer with great honor for the remainder of his tour. To all the officers serving under command of Captain Dake, we say thanks—especially Captain Bonfoey who led our assault landings.")

July-August 1944—Insoemanai Island, Dutch New Guinea

During July and August of 1944 the 1st Fighter Control Squadron completed their facility and the unit stayed at *Insoemanai* with operations running smoothly. The area was now free from serious danger of immediate enemy action and only one *red alert* was called in the month of August. The soldiers rendered valuable assistance in operations to locate missing aircraft and effect rescues.

Under their operational code name, *Wrecker Crystal*, the 1st Fighters steered several lost planes to their bases, issued code messages for air strikes, advised adjacent sectors of aircraft movements, gave out weather information, and maintained 24 hour alert with defensive fighter aircraft.

During August 1944, seventy-seven men were promoted. On 15 August the first issue of beer was received, and on the evening of the 16th a squadron party was held, featuring games of chance like roulette, blackjack, dice, chick-a-luck, and wheels of fortune. Each soldier received fifty free tickets, valued at one Dutch guilder per one-hundred fifty tickets turned in by the winners. Cheese sandwiches and two bottles of beer were provided each man.

Camp was so permanent now that the mess halls had concrete floors and a recreation hall for enlisted men was opened 19 August, formally dedicated with coffee and cake. It featured Ping-Pong tables, various games and writing tables. During the first month Special Services ran twenty movies. The library was stocked with 703 books. Fifty-five of the soldiers were enrolled in correspondence courses, Spanish classes were held, and daily news and war progress maps were posted on the bulletin board.

On 23 August eight of the 1st Fighters were flown to Owi Island to appear before the Officer Candidate Board: Technical Sergeants Bell and Johnson, Staff Sergeant Cowan, Sergeants Free and Veile, and Corporals Jones, Lacy, and Patten.

September 1944—Insoemanai, Dutch New Guinea

The month of September found the squadron still on Insoemanai in Dutch New Guinea, but operational activity was noticeably diminishing. Strikes on Palau and the Halmaheras Islands were made by two of their bomber groups prior to moving up. By month's end only one radar station was operating, but the unit continued to perform the valuable tasks of air-sea rescue support, and steering wayward and distressed aircraft home.

But too soon the 1st Fighter Control Squadron would leave the "good life" on *Insoemanai* behind.

October 1944—Alerted for Movement

During early October 1944, traffic on the Wakde airstrip dropped steadily as first the fighter aircraft, then the bombers moved to more advance bases. Mainland fighting continued and 105mm and smaller weapons firing was heard often. Stories of Japanese resistance and counter-attacks around Maffin Bay and Sarmi were rampant. Douglas A-20 *Havoc* light bombers from Hollandia flew over the unit daily, giving air support to the troops fighting there.

On 14 October the 1st Fighters were alerted for movement to the Philippines. Portable buildings, including the orderly room and dispensary, were dismantled and crated. The plotting board was repainted for the San Jose area in southwestern Mindoro, Philippine Islands.

The 32nd Fighter Sector, of which the 1st Fighter Control Squadron was a vital part, was completed with all installations and in full operation on 26 June 1944, and was closed at 0600 on 21 October 1944.

On 3 November 1944 the unit received orders for water movement to Leyte, Philippine Islands, and sailed 6 November.

One soldier noted,

"The Japs gave us some trouble en route ..."

Kamikaze Attacks

Chapter Six

Invasion of LEYTE
Philippine Islands

4 November 1944

On 4 November, *USS George F. Elliott*, and *USS Capricornus*, arrived at *Insoemanai* and six officers and one-hundred fifty enlisted men from the 1st Fighter Control Squadron went aboard as a loading detail. All loading was done by LCT (Landing Craft, Tank) and LCM (Landing Craft, Mechanized). The soldiers received their pay for October that afternoon. The last meal on the island was breakfast on 6 November. The 1st Fighter Control Squadron was assigned to Hold 3 on the troop transport Elliot, with adequate facilities. After "a very good Navy meal" the ship sailed at 1730 for Hollandia where it anchored for two days in the harbor. The ship's store would not accept the soldiers' Dutch guilders so they were allowed to go ashore and convert the money.

9 November 1944

At noon *USS George F. Elliott* sailed in a convoy of fourteen cargo ships and five destroyers. No air cover was provided, even after a similar size convoy joined up with them on the 12th. At 1600 the convoy was attacked by a Japanese torpedo bomber which was shot down by anti-aircraft fire from the destroyers. It hit the water just two hundred yards from *Elliot* and its already released torpedo went wild, but caused no damage.

14 November 1944

A 1st Fighter soldier recorded his thoughts,

> "Assault landing on Leyte ... under heavy fire and 'kamikaze' attacks did not deter our squadron from performing its assigned duty— all personnel performed with merit."

Staff Sergeant France R. Wanberg,

> "En route from New Guinea to Leyte, we were under a suicide attack by the Japs. It was terrifying to see those planes dive straight at a ship. One plane headed for our LST, but the continuous fire by our anti-aircraft guns shot the plane down just a short distance from our ship. One ship behind us was hit and sunk immediately. We were lucky—the good Lord was on our side once again!"

At 0700 *USS Elliot* anchored in Leyte Gulf and began off-loading men and equipment. Equipment barges off-loaded randomly north of Dulag on *Yellow Beach* and still farther north, causing confusion and scattering the 1st Fighters' supplies and equipment, much of which was damaged or destroyed.

The 1st Fighter Control Squadron's campsite was near the village of San Roque, four miles beyond the unloading point. Due to a shortage of transportation and unloading equipment the men worked until 0300 the next morning. The next day was spent gathering remaining equipment and improving the camp. They were instructed to draw rations at "Base K." When no bread was available the 1st Fighters set up their own bakery, and within two days the kitchen was built and screened, and mess facilities were in place. Power units were promptly installed to furnish light and after several days of hard work the camp "looked very good compared to others in the area." The ground drained well and the unit had coconut trees for shade.

Enemy air raids were frequent, both day and night. While no bombs struck the area directly, foxholes were dug as the danger from anti-aircraft shell fragments was real.

23 November 1944

The presidential promise of Thanksgiving turkey was fulfilled. At 1600 both young turkey and chicken were served with dressing and gravy, sweet potatoes, creamed peas, raisin bread, rolls, and pie.

30 November 1944

Detachment B of the 1st Fighter Control Squadron loaded their equipment for the move to Mindoro—and the D-Day action.

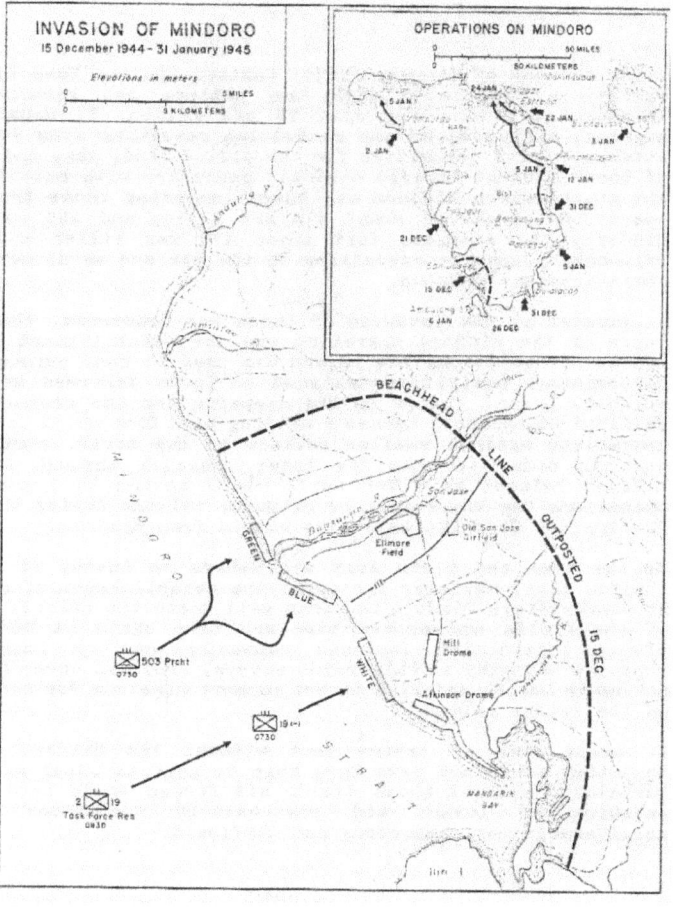

Chapter Seven

MINDORO ISLAND,
Philippine Islands

December 1944

This month started on a negative note. On 6 December, second Lieutenant Martin C, Covington was hit by a spent bullet while lying on his bunk. The .30 caliber bullet entered vertically through the roof of his tent and struck his thigh. The bullet was surgically extracted the following day.

Meanwhile, Detachment A of the 1st Fighter Control Squadron, sat in the harbor at Leyte as D-Day was set back. The 10 officers and 68 enlisted soldiers, **Captain Edward M. Bonfoey** commanding, had prepared for only a few days stay on their LST, and things became increasingly uncomfortable. Sleeping quarters were poorly ventilated and the air soon became foul. Baths and changes of clothing were limited and water faucets were turned on for only a few minutes each morning. Four soldiers were assigned to each bunk on a shift basis—"hot bunk rotation." But most of the men simply slept up on deck.

10 December 1944—Philippines

Bombers of the US 5th Air Force, flying from the island of Leyte, began the pre-invasion hammering of Mindoro Island.

12 December 1944—Philippines

Finally, during the night of 12 December, two task groups from the US 7th Fleet sailed for Mindoro. Fighting continued south of Limon and in the north-west of the island. An American destroyer was damaged off Leyte by a Japanese Kamikaze. In the following days many enemy aircraft were destroyed by escorting US planes and Navy gunfire.

A diary note from a 1st Fighter recorded:

"In five minute intervals, five or six Jap planes would burst into flames and plummet into the ocean. Our guys will retain the vivid memory of fanatical Kamikaze pilots diving their planes steeply to crash into one of our vessels. When they did hit one, terrific explosions resulted followed by flames gutting the ship. We saw great loss of life in these actions."

15 December 1944—D-Day, Mindoro, Philippines

Early the morning of the 15th the convoy reached Mindoro. After a preliminary bombardment of the beachhead, landing of troops from the US 24th Division reinforced by a parachute battalion, commenced at 0735. The landing was carried out immediately south of Luzon in the area of San Agustin.

Captain Bonfoey's Detachment A group landed on *Blue Beach,* while Captain John W. R. Johnson's Detachment B went ashore on *White Beach.* Everyone, regardless of rank, helped to pile cargo on the beaches.

One incident serves to illustrate the enthusiasm of the 1st Fighters,

"When Captain Johnson and Lieutenant Gresham set out in a Jeep to contact Captain Bonfoey, they found the road to *Blue Beach* impassable. They then proceeded up a railroad track toward San Jose town. As they passed a line of plodding men, their leader hailed Captain Johnson and informed him that he and the lieutenant were now ahead of the advance Infantry patrols! Needless to say the two officers turned around and rejoined their troops on the beach where mandatory foxholes dotted the sand by dusk."

During the night many air raids had the men tumbling into their foxholes only to find themselves partially submerged in sea water that appeared with the rising tide.

Sergeant Norman N. Satin,

"We landed under light gunfire and cleared the beach as quickly as we could. We had scores of Jap air raids keeping us always on our toes, and then the raid by the Japanese naval task-force. Bombings and strafing, tracer bullets, ack-ack and searchlights, became a familiar nighttime scene. It was a comforting sight to observe Jap planes blow up in flight or crash to land or sea."

Sergeant Chester Driest provided a narrative to explain how the Squadron operated under combat conditions:

(As was recorded earlier, the Chief Air Controller, an officer, had the responsibility to call red alerts when an approaching flight was determined to be an enemy—or should be considered as one.)

"When the controller called a red alert, it was signaled to the forces on the beachhead by one shot from an anti-aircraft gun. All lights went out, of course, and most activity ceased except in the control center. At the time of the initial landing the control center was set up in a large tent with black out curtains over the entrance. After the beachhead was well established, a few days later, the center was set up in a large shack or shed, also with blackout provisions. The men in the center were usually relaxed as they went about their work, but when the controller called a red alert everyone became instantly tense and alert, and all eyes were focused on the plotting board trees that represented the incoming enemy force.

"It was something to see … the immediate transformation." He continued, "Also on the platform were officers representing friendly forces such as the anti-aircraft gun batteries, the ground controllers who scrambled our fighter aircraft and guided them by radio to the approaching enemy planes, giving our fighter planes a vector (compass heading) toward the enemy, correcting it periodically as needed. They also provided the altitude of the enemy flight and approximate number in the flight. When our fighter plane pilots sighted the enemy force their leader would call, 'Tally Ho." At that point the fight was theirs and our controller's immediate work was done."

The platform contingent included an identification officer, whose job it was to identify the approaching aircraft. This officer was equipped with knowledge of the flight plans of our friendly aircraft in the area and was advised by the radar stations as to whether the radar signal was consistent with our IFF (Identification, Friend or Foe) code.

Plotting Table—Mindoro

Sergeant Driest continued,

"If the enemy planes got though our fighter force, or otherwise managed to approach the vicinity of the beachhead without detection, it was the job of the anti-aircraft guns to deal with them. They were already on alert from the call of red alert earlier. One problem was the 'security perimeter.' If an aircraft entered this zone with the proper IFF code the rules prohibited the guns from firing—which was good for our pilots. But sometimes, as happened one night over Mindoro, the guns were silenced by a friendly plane in the area at the same time a Jap plane flew in.

"Another time our night fighter planes repeated violated the security perimeter in pursuit of an enemy aircraft. Finally, under instructions of the commanding general, our controller ordered the pilot 'in the clear on the radio' that the next time he violated the perimeter he would be 'shot down.' Up until then the Japs had a field day—or night—

shooting up the airstrip. Then our guns were freed up from the 'friendly incursion rule' and blew them away.

"At night we usually had night fighters as an additional weapon with which to combat enemy planes. (Ed. Usually the Northrop P-61 Black Widow) When enemy aircraft were identified far enough away from the beachhead, a night fighter controller located in a van at some distance from our control center, would vector the American aircraft onto the tail of the approaching Japanese plane. When the night fighter's radar fixed on the Jap plane he called, "Tally Ho" and took over from the ground controller.

"At Mindoro one of our area controllers had the unusual experience of controlling our aircraft against an attacking Jap naval task force instead of their airplanes, relaying orders from the commanding general of the local air forces to the pilots of our planes. For this fight we had both night and day fighters, and bombers. Our controller instructed them to stay away from the Jap cruisers and concentrate on the six destroyers in the task force. All enemy vessels received damage, but only one was sunk—a destroyer given the coup de grace by a PT boat after it had been roughed up by our planes."

Throughout the control center operation the emphasis was on speed of decision making. Area controllers were usually First and Second Lieutenant, but had the decision authority of much higher ranks.

When enemy air forces were identified approaching the beachhead area there was no time for a commanding general to consult with his G-3 or other staff to decide which defenses should be activated. The decision for a red alert and the actions it incited had to be made instantaneously. After the first hectic days of a beach landing, shift after shift of controllers could often go without an incident. Without constant activity, generals and colonels could not be assigned to such ignominious boredom—but captains and lieutenants could.

The airmen performed vitally essential roles of keeping the visual information on the plotting board up to the minute, assisting the ground controllers as they guided day and night fighter planes. They also recorded the flight paths on both approaching enemy flights and friendly defensive aircraft. But probably the most essential of all squadron activities was radio communications. This was led by an officer, but performed by the largest number of personnel in all specialties.

Earlier in the book it was mentioned that a Navy controller accompanied the 1st Fighter condition at Hollandia, controlling Navy aircraft from carriers in the operation. After the Hollandia landings, however, General MacArthur's forces could not "borrow" any aircraft carriers and had to depend on the Army Air Corp planes flying from forward airstrips and bases to protect the beachheads.
Surprisingly, the fighter planes were often controlled by the 1st Fighter controllers operating from the CICs of Navy destroyers. Several of their

officers were assigned in such actions as Biak, Noemfoors, and Morotai.

One of their officers, Lieutenant LaBrache, was serving in this capacity aboard USS Nashville when a kamikaze dived into it with disastrous results to the ship and personnel—133 sailors were killed and 190 wounded.

Sergeant Driest notes,

"Reflecting the resourcefulness of our squadron, several of the 1st Fighters who participated in the Biak operation were transferred to the 5297th Airborne Fighter Control Squadron, including Ernest W. Miller, Peter Zidnak, and Melvin Hall. The 5297th was the first flying fighter control squadron in the SW Pacific Theater and a forerunner of the famous AWACs of today.

"There is a lot more detail to our mission, but I've outlined here the most obvious tasks."

Ed. Note: While the squadron was at Brisbane being re-equipped from loses in the sinking of SS Cape San Juan, some personnel went on ahead to New Guinea, including Sergeant Driest, and served as aircraft spotters overlooking a Japanese airfield at Hollandia, where they subsequently landed. Other personnel were sent to Finschhafen to augment 5th Air Force personnel in preparing for the arrival of the main body of the 1st Fighter Control Squadron.

16-31 December 1944— Mindoro, Philippines

On D-Day +1, Captain Bonfoey's Detachment A of the 1st Fighters set up a temporary sector in a San Jose bowling alley. Officers of both A and B Detachments and most of the non-commissioned officers billeted in nearby houses, and the mess was set up in a warehouse. This was only temporary "comfort" as on 23 December operations moved to the hills with cots set up under the trees.

Air raids continued nightly and on 24 December a Japanese naval task force—a battleship, heavy cruiser and six destroyers—approached the northern tip of Mindoro from the west and followed the coastline southward. Within thirty miles American aircraft began strafing the ships and two destroyers were set afire. Still they came and, at 2340, the enemy ships commenced shelling the San Jose airstrip and all but the duty section hit their foxholes.

This sector of the 1st Fighter Control Squadron coordinated allied aircraft activities as they bombed and strafed the Japanese ships. By 0200 on Christmas morning the task force began to withdraw—with three destroyers sunk and the survivors badly damaged.

In the latter half of December the 1st Fighter controllers called nearly one hundred *red alerts* and controlled Allied defensive aircraft in at least as many air raids. Official reports tell of seventy five Japanese planes being shot down with damage to installations and loss of life on Mindoro "light."

The Japanese did manage to sink two Liberty ships and one US destroyer just offshore, with additional surface craft damaged. Favorite targets for the Japanese raids were the PT boat base and the San Jose airstrip.

Detachments A and B performed their mission creditably in those early days after D-Day, while the main body of the squadron back at Leyte prepared to join them.

For the rest of the 1st Fighters on Leyte the Christmas issue of turkey and three bottles of beer per man arrived too late to be prepared on shore, so the "dinner" was loaded onto the LST waiting to take the men to Mindoro. Sixteen officers and two-hundred thirty three enlisted men of the 1st Fighter Control Squadron boarded LST 753 at 1600 on Christmas Day and enjoyed their holiday meal.

With a total of six-hundred fifty troops aboard over half of them had to find sleeping room on deck, under and around their chained down vehicles. The Navy provided them with two meals per day, and after two days bobbing in the Leyte Gulf waters the convoy set sail.

Consisting of four Liberty ships, twenty-two LSTs (Landing Craft, Tanks), seven LCIs (Landing Craft, Infantry), twenty-five escorting destroyers, and a swarm of PT Boats, the convoy sailed south down the Leyte coast before turning northwest toward Mindoro.

All went well and quiet under a rainy, drizzling overcast sky that first day. Then promptly at 0600 on 28 December the war caught up to the 1st Fighters. *General Quarters* sounded as a flight of Japanese aircraft attacked. This first wave was followed at 1030 by a larger force dropping bombs and including Kamikazes. An LST was lost and a Liberty ship set afire and forced to return to Leyte.

A soldier noted,

"Just five-hundred yards behind our LST another Liberty ship was hit by a Kamikaze and exploded with a terrific detonation. Our Corporal William J. Missler was killed instantly by a large piece of metal shrapnel as he tried to dive for cover on the deck of our ship. Sergeant James L. Bennos received a scalp wound and Private First Class Herman A. Tucci was hit in the left shoulder. 2nd Lieutenant Theodore S. Bladykas was injured when a heavy ship's door slammed shut on his right leg. We buried Corporal Missler at sea."

At 1220, eight Navy planes arrived for air cover and they got the *all clear*. Six Japanese aircraft were shot down that day. The Japanese had dropped floating mines among the ships during their raid and at 1845 one exploded and damaged an LST directly behind the 1st Fighter's craft. (*The LST managed to complete the mission to Mindoro with ten feet of water sloshing around in its deck tank.*)

The fight was not over for the ships. On 29 December they were attacked by a much larger force of Japanese aircraft. Despite valiant air cover by American P-61 *Black Widows*, and later by P-47 *Thunderbolts*, and P-38 *Lightnings*, the attack lasted over three hours. At 1700 a Japanese Kamikaze dove for the 1st Fighter's LST and was shot down just off their stern by the ship's gunners.

"I will never forget that attack. I was at the fantail of our LST when the two-seater missed us so narrowly that I could plainly see the expressions on the faces of the Jap pilots."

Enemy aircraft continued to attack, alternately from different quadrants, for another four hours before the *all clear* sounded—then returned at 2220 for another seventy minutes of attacks. The next day from just after midnight until dawn the attacks resumed. By that time Mindoro was in plain sight and US fighter aircraft were flying cover for the convoy. Final score for the "running gun battle" was twenty-five Japanese planes shot down by the ship's anti-aircraft gunners, four downed by American day fighters, and two by night fighters.

Sergeant Chester Driest,

"… the (enemy) task force shot up the airstrip so badly that our controller, Captain Carpenter (Lawrence A.), was given instructions by the Air Force commanding general to order the planes to make for Leyte, rather than trying to land on Mindoro. The pilots followed orders and some of them ran out of gas and had to ditch in the sea before reaching Leyte.

"One pilot called the controller over the air and told him his plane was too badly shot up to make it to Leyte. He asked that a searchlight be turned on and pointed straight up in the air so that he could find his way to the airstrip and land. The controller complied, but heard nothing further. The next morning he called the operations tent and asked about the pilot, and was informed that the pilot had crashed and died attempting to land his crippled plane."

The 1st Fighter Control Squadron finally landed on *Blue Beach* at 0800 on the 30th and the month (and year) ended the next day with campsite preparations and hauling of equipment up from the beach.

Japanese air raids continued nightly.

P-61 Black Widow Night Fighter on an enemy tail.

During this battle there were P-61 fighters operating on the 25th and 26th of December 1944, destroying four enemy aircraft. All Japanese aircraft destroyed from 15 through 29 December in our area totaled 65.

Serving in theater during this time were the 418th, 421st, 547th, and 550th Night Fighter Squadrons of the Fifth Air Force.

Sergeant Chester Driest,
"Yes, we of the 1st Fighter Control Squadron do remember this Christmas season

of 1944—and for our involvement in this section, our squadron received a recommendation for a unit citation from the 310th Bomb Wing."

MILITARY NEWS BULLETIN OF THE ARMED FORCES DATELINE ALLIED HEADQUARTERS IN THE PACIFIC 28 DECEMBER 1944

Since 20 December allied aircraft based on Mindoro, an island lying south of Luzon, have destroyed 114,000 tons of enemy shipping, including 3 Jap destroyers, and shot down or damaged more than 100 Nip planes, it was disclosed yesterday.

Between 15 and 29 December, however, Mindoro itself was battered more heavily by Jap planes than any other similar Allied Pacific base in a comparable period. The Nips flew a total of 344 sorties over Mindoro in that period, or an average of 23 daily. But many of the Nip planes failed to return to their bases.

January 1945—Mindoro, Philippine Islands

New Year's Day 1945 found the 1st Fighters setting up a permanent camp four miles east of San Jose Village on Mindoro. The work to clear the area was intensive, and at 1600 a dinner of fresh turkey, dressing and all the trimmings was served at the temporary mess. Continuous enemy air raids during the first week kept the soldiers busy—in any spare time—improving their shallow foxholes hastily dug upon arrival. Waiting for a bulldozer to be freed up delayed the construction of permanent buildings.

On 5 January 1945, three officers and seventeen soldiers departed for a spot near the town of Bongabong in southeastern Mindoro to establish a GCI station—Ground Control Intercept—to guide interceptor aircraft toward unidentified intruders picked up on the unit's radar. The unit, designated *Buckshot*, went operational with 1st Lieutenant Kirgan commanding.

Back at the main base the new sector building was ready for operation on 17 January, and was immediately recognized as the best set up for its mission anywhere in V Fighter Command. During that month, ninety-four "homings" were accomplished by the 1st Fighters *August Crystal* VHF (Very High Frequency) installation, and thirty-six *red alerts* were called by the control center. The allied forces landing at Lingayen Gulf on Luzon immediately decreased the Mindoro raids drastically.

On 24 January 2nd Lieutenant Covington rejoined the squadron after his hospitalization and was awarded a Purple Heart for his injuries on 6 December.

By 28 January most of the permanent buildings were complete, including a concrete floor and cloth ceiling in the mess hall, and exterior landscaping by the locals.

> "Buying fresh corn with the squadron fund helped meals considerably and two beer issues of four bottles each were greeted with enthusiasm."

The air raids by Japanese forces during January were significant. Listing only a few of them illustrates the point:

On New Year's Day, two Japanese planes—one a twin engine bomber—killed eleven men and wounded ten others in the camp area near the airstrip.

On 3 January, fifteen enemy aircraft flew in very low from different directions at intervals to attack the PT boat base and the airstrip—one American wounded, two P-38 *Lightnings* and an A-20 *Havoc* light bomber destroyed, and twenty-two other aircraft damaged.

The next day, three *Zeros* (Mitsubishi A6M) and a *Betty* (Mitsubishi G4M bomber) attacked shipping and the PT boat base. The *Betty* crash dived into an ammunition ship, completely destroying it with an unknown number of Navy sailors killed.

"The attack on the ammo ship was on the 4th of the month—and it was already our eighteenth *red alert!*"

Corporal Augusta L. Bray adds a very human view to the experience,

"Thinking back on Mindoro, it seems like we were constantly under alert or attack from sea and air. I remember being assigned at night to a machine gun set up below our camp on a fork in the creek. We thought it to be ridiculous, but we set the gun up on a tripod and waited. That night a Jap plane strafed nearby and we decided maybe we ought to dig in and get below the ground surface. We dug a little hole and put a row of sandbags around it. The next night flak fell all around us so we decided we might have to cover the gun. We dug deeper, adding three rows of sandbags and a cover over our hole. That night the Japs dropped the first phosphorous bomb—so we dug a little deeper and added two more layers of sandbags on top. The next morning after the Jap naval bombardment we had to stand on an ammunition box to see out of our machine gun hole!

We certainly saw some good fighter plane dogfights—especially since our side won."

CONFIDENTIAL

HEADQUARTERS
1ST FIGHTER CONTROL SQUADRON
APO 321
200.6   15 January 1945

SUBJECT: **RECOMMENDATION FOR UNIT CITATION**

TO: COMMANDING OFFICER, 310TH BOMB WING,
          APO 321 (ATTENTON: A-1 SECTION)

1. In compliance with letter, your Headquarters, file and subject as above, dated 1 Jan 1945, and also with reference to War Department Circular No. 333, dated 22 Dec 1943, an accounting of the actions of this organization during the recent shelling by the Japanese Naval Task Force on 26 Dec 1944 is submitted herein:

On the afternoon of 26 December 1944, a Japanese Task Force consisting on one battleship, one heavy cruiser, and six destroyers, was sighted in the waters off Mindoro Island on a course which threatened the security of the beachhead. The Task Force was kept under surveillance by our aircraft, and its actions and position reported to the sector every few minutes. The Bomb Wing alerted every available aircraft and organized them into bombing and staffing units.

The enemy force approached the northwest tip of Mindoro and turned south, heading directly for the Mindoro beachhead. At a point 35 miles northwest of San Jose our aircraft began strafing the enemy fleet. Almost immediately two destroyers were set afire. The enemy was under constant attack by our air forces from that time until early the next morning.

At 2340 hours of the same day the enemy warships began to shell the area which included the airstrip. After over a half hour's bombardment the enemy forces turned and retreated into the China Sea, still under attack by our bombers and fighters.

During this entire period the sector (*Ed. Note: "sector" refers to the 1st Fighter Control Squadron's operation*) collected information from our aircraft concerning the location and activities of the enemy and passed this information immediately to Brigadier General Hutchinson who remained in constant communication with the sector. The sector assisted attacking aircraft to find the enemy warships. When the aircraft were out of ammunition, the sector directed them to Leyte, or if the planes were shot up or short of gas, assisted them in landing at our air strips.

The personnel on duty at the sector remained steadfast at their posts during the

Japanese shelling, despite the fact that the sector operations tent was completely unprotected against shelling or bombing attacks, there being neither sandbags nor an earthen embankment affording any measure of protection. Although the personnel wore helmets, this seemed as only unconvincing moral support. To those in the sector tent the shells seemed to be landing uncomfortably close, yet no one abandoned their post for the greater safety of a foxhole. Personnel on duty at the GCI station, located in the midst of the area subjected to the bombardment, performed their duties courageously and placed the safety of the sector before their own.

The personnel of the 1st Fighter Control Squadron on duty during this emergency did everything possible to insure the safety of the Mindoro beachhead by properly disseminating al intelligence information as fast as it was secured, and by using their every facility in assisting the air defense against the Japanese task force, regardless of personal safety.

FOR THE COMMANDING OFFICER:
Rhinehart H. Miller, Captain, Air Corps
Adjutant

February 1945—Mindoro, Philippine Islands

By early February things were "100% better" on Mindoro with the Japanese now concentrating their attacks elsewhere. 1st Lieutenant Theodore S. Bladykas, who had served with the 1st Fighters for only nine months, but been in theater for three years, received his orders to return to the United States.

On 6 February, Lieutenant White and five enlisted men left for detached duty at Clark Field, Luzon. On the 12th, ten men with Technical Sergeant Jack A. Walker in charge went to Apo Island to put D/F (direction finding) station #2 into operation.

It was a good month for promotions, especially for the officers of the 1st Fighter Control Squadron. The commanding officer (Dake) promoted to major, and most of the 2nd and 1st lieutenants moved up a grade.

March 1945—Mindoro, Philippine Islands

The squadron remained on Mindoro with no enemy air raids or *red alerts*. All precautions were fully observed because there was still the possibility of attacks at any time. But the soldiers were far from idle.

During a single week ending 17 March, the 1st Fighter Control Squadron's control center tallied twenty-nine thousand radar reports—the highest weekly total ever turned in by a single Fighter Control Center in the Southwest Pacific during WWII, as reported by the 85th Fighter Wing. *August Crystal* had one-hundred eleven "homings" during March.

April 1945—Mindoro, Philippine Islands

The squadron continued smooth operation of the 42nd Fighter Control Center on Mindoro at a time when enemy attacks became less and less likely. No *red alerts* were called. A letter of commendation arrived from the Commanding General, V Fighter Command and the Commanding Officer, 85th Fighter Wing praising all 1st Fighter Control Squadron personnel on operational improvements made and the high standards of efficiency reached in the flow of accurate information from their center. Much of the squadron's work during this time involved critical air-sea rescue communications and Navy officers sent many formal letters of "thanks."

Typical air-sea actions include:

10 April—report of an airman in the water a mile west of the airstrip, flashing a mirror. Two planes and a crash boat dispatched to the area found debris, but not the flier.

12 April—life jackets with dye markers reported. Sent two fighter aircraft and a PBY *Catalina*. Three fliers located in a skiff, and a crash boat picked them up.

13 April—a fighter plane crashed into the sea. Another plane dropped two life rafts at the scene. A PT boat sent out found the rafts, but no survivors. Such reports were almost daily during the month.

May 1945—Mindoro, Philippine Islands

In May, ASR (*Adjusted Service Rating*) scores, used to sequence rotation of troops back home, were posted. Four 1st Fighter officers and ten enlisted men qualified with eighty-five or more points.

On 21 May, Major Dake was informed that the squadron would be once again divided to operate two sectors: Mindoro (later changed to Lingayen) and Laoag.

June 1945—Mindoro, Philippine Islands

During the month of June the new orders were put into effect. The Headquarters section of the 1st Fighters would operate the 45th Fighter Control Center at Lingayen, and Detachment A took over the 43rd Fighter Control Center at Laoag. Advance echelons were sent to the two locations to prepare for the scheduled air movements of troops and equipment.

The month on Mindoro closed out with the squadron assisting in twenty-two air-sea rescues, and *August Crystal* accomplishing two-hundred twenty-two successful "homings."

Memories of Mindoro

Anonymous,
"The war in the South Pacific was pretty much a dry war. Booze had to be imported from wherever, but we each got a ration every

few months of beer, or if we were lucky, some wine. Some guys sold their ration, others drank one bottle of beer each Saturday until it was gone, and still others sat right down and drank it all at once and got it over with.

"Some of the guys made their own with grain they got in packages from the States. Then on Mindoro, some fellows devised an icing tank and for a price you could check in your beer, and when you figured it was cold, check it out again—not the same beer, but the same number of bottles. Some wise-guys got the idea of drinking their beer, then refilling the bottles with water and recapping them. Then they checked them into the tank, later checking the same number of bottles out—of somebody else's beer. You can see why the icing tank didn't stay in business very long."

Sergeant Chester Driest,
"Mindoro was a minor operation as far as war engagements were concerned. But the Japanese mounted dozens of bomber attacks upon us for the first several days, until our fliers finished knocking them out of the air, and our forces landed on Luzon"

Chapter Eight

Laoag and Lingayen

July 1945—Laoag and Lingayen, Philippines

After some weather delays, airlifts moving the 1st Fighters to the new Control Center locations on Laoag and Lingayan were completed 3 and 8 July respectively.

Captain Kennickell and a team of eighteen soldiers had arrived at Laoag on 23 June ahead of the airlift and had the sector building well under way when the others arrived.

1st Fighter Control Squadron Detachment A took over operations on 10 July 1945 and were visited by the Commanding General of the Philippines Air Defense Command that day, relating his pleasure with the progress the 1st Fighters had made in such a short time. Adding to the morale lifter, permission was received to rehabilitate a downtown building into an Enlisted Men's Club—dubbed *Club Ilocana.*

At Lingayen, the main body of the squadron assumed operational control of the 45th Fighter Control Center on 9 July.

At the end of July, First Sergeant Marcus J. Blome, the first soldier assigned to the new forming 1st Fighter Control Squadron in January 1942, Technical Sergeant James R. Bell and Sergeant Leonard J. O'Connor completed their war duty and returned to the United States.

6 August 1945—Atomic Bomb Dropped on Japan

14 August 1945—Japan Surrenders

August 1945—Laoag and Lingayen, Philippines

(*Author's Note: microfilm for August operations of the 1st Fighter Control Squadron is virtually unreadable. The following narrative is what could be deciphered with a magnifying glass.*)

The Atomic Bomb and Japan's capitulation had conversations centered on the historic events, mixed with rumors of how soon they would be able to go home. Enlisted soldiers completed their club facilities at both Laoag and Lingayen. Dances became regular events and some of the men were entertained in civilian homes, at parties in provincial buildings, schoolhouses, and municipal halls. "The Filipino love for formal programs and long speeches became quite evident at these affairs."

There is one experience on Lingayen reported by a soldier that is an uplifting event in the war:

Staff Sergeant France Wanberg,
"One night we went to see the stage play *Oklahoma*. After the performance I became separated from the other men. They called out my name, Wanberg!

"Unbeknownst to me, it happened that my uncle who was in the Navy was also at the show. When he heard the name Wanberg, he thought to himself, 'I bet that is my nephew, France.' The next time he had leave from his ship anchored in Lingayen Gulf he started looking for me. He went to every camp in the area, finally coming to ours. He went into the orderly room and asked if they had a France Wanberg, and they directed him to my tent. What a surprise when he walked into our tent!

"A few days later we got together, found a small café, ordered two steaks (actually water buffalo—and tough), and got a bottle of Philippine wine and had a great afternoon visiting and talking about our families. That was something when an uncle and nephew got together over 8,000 miles from home!"

September 1945
Laoag and Lingayen, Philippines

The 70th Fighter Squadron continued to operate at Laoag, but no US military aircraft flew from Lingayen in September. The war was over, but vigilance was still the order of the day. Air-sea rescue work was as heavy as ever, and Navy PB4Y aircraft continued their daily search missions. "Homing steers" decreased markedly to just sixteen in September—down from sixty-one in August.

Bad weather with typhoon strength winds hampered flight traffic between Luzon and Okinawa. Occupation troops were flown north, while rescued POWs flew south to Manila.

The soldiers of the 1st Fighter Control Squadron speculated on their return home after a revision in the "point system" made nearly all who had shipped over on SS Cape San Juan eligible by 1 October 1945.

The exodus actually began in September with those 1st Fighters with eighty-five points, followed by those over thirty-eight years of age, getting orders on 18 September—nine officers and one-hundred enlisted. By the 23rd, anyone over thirty-five was on the way home.

The squadron CO, Major Donald Dake was among the returnees and Captain Kennickell assumed command. Many adjustments in duties among remaining personnel were needed in order to continue operations efficiently.

First Sergeant duties passed through many hands, with Staff Sergeant Myslenski winding up in the spot by month end.

The 1st Fighters from Laoag travelled by airplane, jeep, weapons carriers, or 6x6 trucks, to Lingayen where service records were examined, immunization records updated, and equipment turned in. The Lingayen Enlisted Club became the scene of joyous celebrations by those with orders for returning home. Trucks carried the lucky ones to the Manila Replacement Depot.

At long last Purple Hearts were awarded to the 1st Fighters injured during the Cape San Juan disaster, and unofficial word came that the Lingayen Sector would be shut down.

Quote from September's Squadron Report:
"Life is not much changed from previous months except for those who have been transferred to Manila from outlying stations, and for those who have left on that happy eastward boat ride. Some of us are conditioning ourselves to the life of rear-area commandos by learning to live in barracks rather than tents, and to get our beer more regularly. Aside from the big administrative changes, the month for most of us has been just another phase of the 'sweating-it-out' period, slightly mitigated by the steps taken to increase our comfort."

October 1945—Manila/Laoag/Leyte/Palawan

At the beginning of October, 1st Fighter personnel were still at Lingayen and Laoag, Philippine Islands, but by month's end their Headquarters was at Fort McKinley, Manila, with detachments at Laoag, Leyte and Palawan.

The squadron got another new commanding officer and dozens of key positions were taken by new men. "High point" men were transferred from the 1st Fighter Control Squadron to the 8th FCS for shipment home. The Lingayen control center was abandoned,

133

and on 15 October the 1st Fighter Control Squadron officially transferred to Manila and was placed under the 13th Fighter Control Command. Principle tasks still involved "homing" and coordination of air-sea rescue, with small units operating stations from Laoag to Zamboanga.

November 1945—Same Stations
(Microfilm totally unreadable)

December 1945—Swan Song for the 1st Fighters

The final month of 1945, four long years after the attack on Pearl Harbor, was the last for the 1st Fighter Control Squadron as a WWII organization.

"After serving with skill and honor through the New Guinea and Philippines campaigns—and having established itself as the LAST operational fighter control squadron in the Philippines—the 1st Fighter Control Squadron was finally 'put on the shelf' for a well-deserved rest."

The air-sea rescue duties were now duplicated by other units and on 13 December 1945 the remaining personnel were transferred to the 595th Signal Air Warning Battalion.

"Time to say, WELL DONE."

1ST FIGHTER CONTROL SQUADRON

A Roster of Personnel Who Sailed Aboard SS Cape San Juan in 1943.

Those noted in bold were lost KIA in the torpedo sinking of the ship 11 November 1943—or as indicated.

CAPTAINS

Magee, George J.
McBride, Irwin C.
Miller, Rhinehart H.
Rickman, Samuel M.

1st LIEUTENANTS

Bonfoey, Edward M.
Breen, James M.
Coon, William L.
Garst, Kenneth L.
Hugh, George F.
Hurlburt, John w. R.
Johnson, Wendell C.

2nd LIEUTENANTS

Burks, Robert F.
Carpenter, Lawrence A.
Case, Robert N.
Coil, Stanley F.
Croom, George J.
Evenson, Obert
George, Jimmy
Kennickell, Alfred R.
Kimball, Richard P.
Kleeger, Raymond M.
Kohnhorst, Maurice L.

Kornfeld, Jerome J.
McCormick, Robert J.
McDonald, Stanley
O'Sullivan, Marcellus
Rosenberger, Ralph C.

MASTER SERGEANTS

Blome, Marcus J.
Bullock, Harry J.
Plotner, Charles E.

TECH. SERGEANTS

Bartlett, Wilson E.
Bell, James R.
Berkey, Arthur K.
Christenson, Arnold
Cox, James L.
Drankie, John R.
Ferrell, Duane W.
Humphries, Troy T.
Johnson, Earl W.
Kinkade, John M.
Slay, Kenneth P.
Sorrells, Lester E.
Williamson, Mitchell
Woods, Harley G.

STAFF SERGEANTS

Adams, James T.
Barthels, Henry Jr.
Butz, Warren W.
Cooper, Paul E.
Coulter, William M.
Dowling, Warren H.
Farmer, Frank T.
Fuller, Layton C.
Hartley, Thomas J.
Hudgens, Howard H.
Jones, Virgin A.
Kiplinger, Philip Jr.
Lawrence, Charles M.
Leary, Bruce P.
Lords, Francis V.
Leutkemeyer, Clarence
McKenna, John W.
Megalonakis, George
Miller, Ernest W.
Nergenah, Alpha L.
Nichols, Thomas J. Jr.
Opp, Williard
Pearson, Edwin G.
Reede, James J.
Rizzuto, Leonard F.
Tangye, Aaron J. Jr.
Tedrick, Robert D.
Viktor, Joseph J.

Walker, Jack A.
Wanberg, France R.
Wells, Thomas E.
Zdinak, Pete

SERGEANTS

Bartholomew, Wm R.
Baumgartner, William C.
Bennos, James L.
Bonkoski, Edward L.
Brandt, William L.
Burt, Herman L.
Cannon, Edmund A
Chapman, Howard N.
Clowdus, James C.
Comelia, Patrick A.
Considine, Willam E.
Cotter, Patrick A.
Cowan, James T.
Dell, Joe W.
Driemeyer, Edward D.
Driest, Chester W.
Dunn, Robert J.
Dvorak, Joseph J.
Fadness, Paul R.
Faler, George S.
Fortman, Gilbert C.
Free, William J.
Frost, Donald P.

137

Goldberg, Leo
Goe, Yem S.
Henry, William H.
Horominski, Stanley
Hunter, Jessie R.
Ingo, Lawrence J.
Johnson, Gilbert C.
Krambeer, Clifford J.
Krivacek, Steve
Levin, Morris J.
Loeb, Stephen H.
McCurry, Alfred C.
McCurry, Malcolm R.
McNary, Herbert A.
McQuaide, Marry E.
Mellert, Carl W.
Muslenski, Albin J.
Nail, Olan P.
Nekuda, John
O'Conner, Thomas F. Jr.
Patterson, Warren E.
Paul, Joseph L.
Pieper, Paul T.
Poole, Phillip A.
Price, Harvey J.
Raymond, Gordon N.
Rice, George F.
Satin, Norman N.
Schmitt, Raymond E.
Schrandt, Clotus W.

Schutawie, Samuel J.
Scott, Harvey B.
Schock, Walter R.
Shroat, Reginald G.
Skinner, David T.
Sullivan, Carl J.
Thommes, Arnold A.
Veile, Ernest A.
Watts, Vernon L.
Zelman, Robert

CORPORALS

Akers, Duane R.
Altuna, Arthur
Barger, Wilbur A.
Barratt, Lawrence
Baughman, Robert E.
Baxter, Harold G.
Bettasso, Bernard J.
Braciak, Leonard W.
Bramlet, Grover M.
Bray, Augusta L.
Bray, Paul C.
Breitwieser, Clyde R.
Chaney, Quintin E.
Citron, Abbott
Clemmons, John H.
Conroy, Emmet A.
Conti, Carlo V.
Crawford, Don R.

Dalluge, Reuben G.
Dannamaker, Donald
Darsey, Wm L.
Dunn, Thomas F.
Eitzenhofer, Clyde M.
Erickson, Eric W.
Fischer, Benjamin E.
Frankel, David
Fuher, Joseph B. Jr.
Goldberg, Irving J.
Goldberg, Maurice E.
Green, Virgin C.
Hall, Melvin L.
Hankins, Charles M.
Harkness, Vance P.
Hergenrather, R.
Hinesley, Walter C.
Holland, Bernie E.
Howard, Lawernce T.
Hunsley, Henry
Jaca, Frank Jr.
Johnson, George
Jones, Carl W.
Jones, Raymond W.
Jones, Thomas R.
Kjarvonen, Carl E.
Kern, Donald C.
Kisabeth, Gerald W.
Klein, William
Koeppe, John F. Jr.
Kosch, James W.

Kosmyna, John
Lacy, Rex E.
Lindskag, Clifford W.
Lubker, Robert E.
Mallen, William P.
Martin, Earnest W.
McClanahan, David S.
McGinley, Joseph F.
Melhus, Albert M.
Metzger, James F.
Missler, Wm J. (1944)
Moeller, Herman J.
Mortimer, Charles R.
Neuland, Edward J. Jr.
O'Linn, Robert P.
Olson, Roger L.
Owens. O'Brien
Pace, Grover G.
Palonis, Rollin W.
Parciak, Chester E.
Patrick, Rollin W.
Patten, Lawerence
Perani, Peter
Pietras, Chester M.
Pinckley, Herbert Jr.
Prohaska, Richard E.
Putman, Max L.
Reardon, Robert R.
Reed, John D.
Reeder, Van
Roberts, Hubert M.

Rusmisel, Donald
Sidlowski, Peter J.
Slater, Joseph L.
Smyth, Joseph M.
Speiker, Robert J.
Stauffer, Maxwell P.
Stewert, James F. Jr.
Stone, Solomom B.
Steifel, Joe
Tharp, Milton S.
VanVactor, Robert D.
Veno, Albert J.
Vorum, John E.
Walker, Coborn D.
Watson, George E.
Weatherby, Russell M.
Welch, Donald C.
Wilkans, Max F
Wolman, Stanley J.
Wong, Ernest
Zaborowski, Chester
Zumdick, John H. Jr.

PRIVATES
1st CLASS

Bergen, Edwain P.
Bethon, Thomas F.
Bluhm, Franklin A.
Bryce, Robert M.
Browne, Robert B.

Campbell, Warren H.
Carter, John H. Jr
Champagne, Eugene J.
Clark, Robert C.
Coleman, Robert M.
Collins, John E.
Davil, Herschel E.
DiMicco, Albert S.
Doane, Joe L.
Dregno, Kenneth D.
Dunlap, Leslie L.
Dunn, Jerome B.
Durachko, Martin P.
Erdos, Stephen A.
Gartland, Robert E.
Griffin, Martin J.
Halsted, Abner E.
Hoessli, Roland
Holahan, Frank S.
Imel, David W.
Keen, Benjamin
Kelly, Kenneth R.
Klein, Harold T.
Kraft, Casper J.
Manns, Forest
Masonh, Clyde J.
McCullough, Daryle
McCullough, Max H.
McGregor, Harold
McPeak, Elmo
McPhelin, Joseph P.

Miner, Charles E.
Minjares, Phillip A.
Mocciaro, Rosario A.
Morgan, Stanton L.
Morrison, Ethan B.
Nichols, S.M.
O'Conner, Leonard J.
Olmstead, William R.
Padillo, Placido R.
Passmore, Charles D.
Powell, George E.
Rayburn, Sammie B.
Rheume, William L.
Schaechtal, George R.
Schmidt, Edward C.
Scianna, Samuel J.
Sheets, Emmet R.
Smith, Robert B.
Stellato, Anthony N.
Swartz, Robert E.
Szydlowski, Joseph S.
Thoennes, Raymond J.
Tubbs, David G.
Tucci, Herman A.
Tuohy, Paul A.
Twomkey, James B.
Vinikas, Joseph A.
Wagner, Roy W.
Wilson, William H. Jr
Wit, Kurt E.
Wolverton, Donald E.

PRIVATES

Agular, Johhny
Allison, Robert L.
Artiaga, Albert
Babulski, Edward J.
Barnhardt, James W.
Bitting, Willard E.
Cassano, Donato
Champagne, Gordon J.
Cook, Carl Jr
Goopert, Paul T.
Cox, Cecil R.
Curto, Angelo
Decker, William E.
Gong, William A.
Geyer, Francis M.
Gibson, Clarence
Graham, Jean F.
Hakala, Tuano V.
Hanes, Charlie C.
Hess, John J.
Hill, Eliza R.
Honeycutt, James B.
Huio, Lyle
Hunt, William S.
Ingels, Raymond M.
Jefferson, William C.
Kelly, Paul R.
Kies, Adolph H.

Kloda, Francis X.
Kumm, Clayton O.
Lewis, Edgar L.
McCormick, Joseph
McCumber, Charles
McMillen, Delbert J.
Michalak, Joseph
Miller, Peter J.
Moles, Earl
Morgan, Jack G.
Myers, Kenneth M.
Oliver, William H.
Paredes, Willie R.
Payne, George H.
Raddon, Dean A.
Richard, Harold L.
Richards, George E.
Ricicar, Jerome E.
Riley, Paul W.

Rotondella, Louis
Ruiz, Miguel
Schultz, Leonard E.
Sepeda, Amador
Shoup, Paul E.
Smith, Roland D.
Snider, Dolphie C.
Soto, Cecilio S.
Stromborn, Charles K.
Tackett, Billie
Tall, Nathan
Vega, Jesse J.
Vermuele, Arthur F.
Wicker, Ottie E.
Wolman, Stanley J.
Teagott, john A.
Yockey, Morris D.

Biographies

Edward Monroe "Munny" Bonfoey
(1912-1997)

Born November 23, 1912 in Philadelphia, Pennsylvania, Edward Bonfoey was a 1931 graduate of Lawrenceville Preparatory School, Lawrenceville, New Jersey. While at Lawrenceville, he spent six months in Europe with his grandparents, and General and Mrs. Abelardo Rodriguez.

Rodriguez later became Governor of Baja California, and President of Mexico in 1936. During this trip, Bonfoey became fluently bilingual in Spanish.

Bonfoey attended the University Of Virginia Graduate School Of Foreign Languages, earning a Masters Degree in Languages in 1933.

Edward Bonfoey married Sarah Dean Witz of Staunton, VA on October 31, 1936, attended by his parents, four grandparents and Sarah's uncle, Secretary of State Cordell Hull and Mrs. Hull.

From 1936 to 1941 Bonfoey was vice-president of sales for Monroe Chemical Company.

With the onset of WWII, Bonfoey served in the U.S. Army Air Corps from December 12, 1941 to January 1946, discharged at the rank of Major. He was Assault Controller with the 1st Fighter Control Squadron in four D-Day landings in New Guinea and the Philippine Islands. He was torpedoed 11 November 1943 and wounded twice.

After the war, Bonfoey served as president of Monroe Chemical Company, Quincy, IL, then moved to Staunton, VA in December 1947, where he joined the Basic Witz Furniture Industries. He was elected President in 1950, and retired as Chairman of the Board in 1968 upon the sale of the business.

After retirement, Bonfoey spent six months of the year on his yacht *Tae-Foy* in Fort Lauderdale, Florida. He was a 32nd Degree Mason and member of the Episcopal Church.

Edward Monroe Bonfoey died on April 14, 1997 at 84 years old.

Wakde Island New Guinea 1944

Chester Driest
(1920-1999)

Chester Driest was born June 18, 1920, in Detroit, Michigan. As a lad he was interested in Ham Radio. This interest carried over into his service in WWII.

Joining the Army Air Corps in 1942, Driest was assigned to Camp Crowder, Missouri, for a Radio Communications Course with additional training in transmitters and receivers. After finishing school he was transferred to March Field, California, to join the 1st Fighter Control Squadron.

He was part of a small detachment from his squadron who made several D-Day assault landings in the South Pacific and established fighter control centers after the initial combat landings.

Chester Driest received the Purple Heart, the Victory Medal with four Overseas Service Bars, the Asiatic-Pacific Theater Ribbon with three Bronze Battle Stars, the Good Conduct Medal, the Philippine Liberation Medal with one Bronze Battle Star, and the Bronze Service Arrowhead. He finished his service with the rank of Technical Sergeant.

Upon returning home in November 1945, Driest continued to work in communications, retiring as Quality Control Director for Gables Engineering, Coral Gables, FL. Coincidentally, Gable's Engineering developed and manufactured many of the radio control panels and equipment used by Boeing and Pan American.

Driest was a charter member of Good Shepard Lutheran Church, Hernando, Florida, a member of VFW, and an amateur radio operator.

Chester Driest died at age 78 on March 24, 1999, in Hernando, Florida.

Donald A. Dake
(1917-1998)

Donald Dake was born April 1917 in Flint, Michigan. He earned his bachelor's degree from Michigan State University and master's degree from Indiana University.

He served in the Army Air Corps during World War II in the South Pacific as the much revered Commanding Officer of the 1st Fighter Control Squadron, returning to Michigan in 1945 as a Major.
Marrying Marijane Ochs on July 17, 1948, in Lansing, Michigan, they moved to South Bend, IN in 1948 where he served as Superintendent of Schools.

Dake served the South Bend schools for more than forty years as a teacher, administrator, and superintendent before his retirement in 1979. He held the top position in the school system during one of the most challenging decades in the system's history. Becoming superintendent in 1969 at the height of student protests and in an age of racial change, the desegregation of city schools occupied much of Dake's time and talent, and he was known for accomplishing the task without taking a confrontational approach.

He was known for his long-standing support of the arts, and helped form the Michiana Arts and

147

Sciences Council. Dake also worked to promote the efforts of the South Bend Symphony, the Michiana Opera Guild, and the Michiana Public Broadcasting Corp.

During his days with the South Bend schools, Dake was a teacher at John Adams High School, director of pupil personnel for the schools and was a principal at Riley High School. He also served as director of secondary education and assistant superintendent of instruction. In 1988 he was inducted into the South Bend School Boosters Hall of Fame.

The recipient of many major honors for his civic commitment, Dake received the South Bend Rotary Club's Distinguished Community Service Award in 1985. He earned the Michiana Arts and Sciences Council Community Arts Award in 1980 and was honored with a community tribute dinner after his retirement from the school system in 1979. He also served as vice chairman of the board of the South Bend Symphony and as chairman of the board of the Snite Museum of Art.

Dake and his wife, Marijane, were members of the First Baptist Church, South Bend.

Donald A. Dake died Dec. 7, 1998, at age 81.

AUTHOR NOTES

This writer has a personal connection to USAT Cape San Juan ship, having grown up with my father's stories of the sinking of the ship. Her maiden voyage to Townsend, Australia, in 1943, was his first assignment as a newly minted Ensign in the US Maritime Service. His second voyage was coastwise from San Pedro to San Francisco, where he was transferred to the SS Avalon and missed the fateful next voyage to Australia.

After his death in 1992, I had a faint idea about writing about the event, and was trying to find information on the ship and the sinking. Serendipity lent a hand when I ran across a newspaper article about a reunion of soldiers who had experienced the sinking of USAT Cape San Juan.

Chester Driest was the organizer of the event. My call to him in Florida was the seminal event for creating my first novel. After I told him of my connection to the ship he made me an honorary member of the 1st Fighter Control Squadron and sent me the compiled records of the documents, photographs, and memoirs of the group.

It was one comment that he made during our phone conversation that launched the plot for the historical-fiction novel, *Code Name: ORION'S EYE*. He said, "You know, Tom, a lot of the guys in the unit didn't realize how secret our radar equipment was." The resulting story launched the series of Amos Mead Adventures, now up to five books with this writing.

ABOUT THE AUTHOR

Tom Gauthier is a retired business executive with degrees in Business Administration and Psychology. He served in the US Army as a combat intelligence analyst and in the US Air Force Reserve as a C-119 Loadmaster.

He began writing novels in 2008. His first work, **Code Name: ORION'S EYE**, was an outgrowth of his studies with the Long Ridge Writers' Group. As reported in the Author's Notes, his meeting with Chester Driest was equally seminal to the work. It also began the "career" of the character of *Amos Mead*.

In addition to writing, Dr. Gauthier records his novels as Audio Books from his studio in Janesville, CA, under the imprint, ToMar Associates, Publishing. The first, MEAD'S TREK, is available on iTunes, Audible.com, and Amazon.com. This publication of the history and the memories of the 1st Fighter Control Squadron is Dr. Gauthier's first work of non-fiction. Tom is a member of the Military Writers Society of America.

Tom lives in rural northeast California with his wife of forty years, Marlene. Merging a family in 1975, Tom and Marlene enjoy their four children, thirteen grandchildren, and soon to be seventeen great-grandchildren.

BIBLIOGRAPHY

Appelbaum, Albert, Chief Mate, SS Edwin T. Meredith, Interview excerpts.

Archives New Zealand, Wellington, New Zealand - for the images from the photograph album of Number 6 (Flying Boat) Squadron [AIR 144/3 12 page 49].

Berkey, Arthur K., Technical Sergeant, US Army Air Corps, personal notes.

Bonfoey, Edward Monroe, Lieutenant, US Army Air Corps, excerpts from letters home.

Bray, Augusta L., Corporal, US Army Air Corps, essay excerpts

Coulter, William M., Staff Sergeant, US Army Air Corps, essay excerpts

Dake Donald A., quotes excerpted from Loeb essay.

Driest, Barbara and Edie for information and photos of Chester Driest.

Driest, Chester W., 1st Fighter Control Squadron, US Army, excerpts of interviews and essays.

Klein, William, Corporal, US Army Air Corps, essay excerpts

Loeb, Stephen H., Sergeant, US Army Air Corps, essay excerpts.

Miller, Rhinehart H., Captain, US Army Air Corps, Adjutant to CG Army Air Forces, report excerpts, Commendation Letter.

Moss, William T., Captain of Pan Am Mariner PBM-3R, excerpt from report. Essay 'The Day I Drank The Admiral's Whiskey'

Naval History and Heritage Command website for information and images of the Cape San Juan and the USS Dempsey (DE-26).

Pallavsina, Alfred, Salnaggi, Cesare, excerpts from *2194 Days of War*, Galley Books.

Plotner, Charles K., Private, US Army Air Corps, Essay excerpts:

Putnam, Max L., Private, US Army Air Corps, essay excerpts.

Robin, George H., Second Officer Pan Am PBM, sketch.

Rutherford B. Hayes Presidential Center, Colonel Stanley Wolfe Collection - for the images of the survivors arriving in Suva, Fiji.

Salnaggi, Cesare; Pallavsina, Alfred, excerpts from *2194 Days of War*, Galley Books.

Satin, Norman N. "Pops", Sergeant, US Army Air Corps, essay excerpts

Scott, Jenny - Blog about <u>RNZAF No. 6 Squadron</u> participation in rescue of SS Cape San Juan, and her book '<u>DUMBO DIARY Royal New Zealand Air Force No.6 (Flying Boat) Squadron 1943-1945</u>'.

Ship's Log, YMS-241, Minesweeper, excerpts from 12, November 1943

Squadron Report excerpt: 1st Fighter Control Squadron, September 1945.

Stone, Eric: numerous excerpts from research and website www.ssarkansan.com

Thompson, Seymour, Lieutenant USNR, watercolor painting.

Wanberg, France R., Staff Sergeant, US Army Air Corps, essay excerpts

Williamson, Mitchell, Technical Sergeant, US Army Air Corps, essay, *Love Lifted Me,* and compilation of US Government microfilm Records for various historical contexts

OTHER BOOKS BY GAUTHIER

Amos Mead Adventure Series

Code Name: ORION'S EYE
2nd ed., Patriot Media, Inc., Publishers, 2012

MEAD'S TREK
2nd ed., Patriot Media, Inc., Publishers, 2011

DIE LISTE: Revenge on the Black Sun.
1st ed., Patriot Media, Inc., Publishers, 2013

FORCE THREE RISES
1st ed., ToMar Associates, Publishing 2015

Award Winning Novels, Library of Congress

A VOYAGE BEYOND REASON
1st ed., Outskirts Press, 2009

The factual record of "Coach" (CBS TV Survivor) Ben Wade's solo kayak voyage down the west coast from upper Baja California, Mexico, to Colombia, South America, wrapped in a fictional story that drives the suspense of the feat to a climactic ending.

Children's Books

PUMPKINS To HOLLY
1st ed. ToMar Associates, Publishing 2015

Cover Blurb for MEAD'S TREK

"Here's a voice that's original, animated, and refreshing. Tom Gauthier definitely knows what he's writing about—and it shows. You're there, amidst the action, feeling, hearing, even smelling the tension. Enjoy the adventure."
Steve Berry
New York Times and #1 International Best Selling Author

Tom Gauthier books are available on Amazon.com, Kindle, and other web retailers and local bookstores.

Contact:

Dr. Tom Gauthier
ToMar Associates, Publishing
PO Box 362
Janesville, California 96114

www.tomgauthier.com

www.ingramcontent.com/pod-product-compliance
Lightning Source LLC
Chambersburg PA
CBHW071505040426
42444CB00008B/1505